Air Combat
During Arab-Israeli Wars

JAKUB MARSZAŁKIEWICZ

Air Combat
During Arab-Israeli Wars

KAGERO

FIRST EDITION
© by KAGERO Publishing, 2017

AUTHOR
Jakub Marszałkiewicz

EDITORS
Jakub Marszałkiewicz

TRANSLATION/PROOFREADING
Tomasz Basarabowicz

COVER
Łukasz Maj

DTP
Kagero Studio

COLOR PROFILES
Color profiles: Bill Dady, Janusz Światłoń

PHOTO SOURCE
Library of Congress – http://www.loc.gov • IDF 1948 Israel Independence War – http://idf-israel1948.
blogspot.com • Israeli Air Force – http://www.iaf.org.il • Ed Okun "Modeling Military History" –
http://edokunscalemodelingpage.blogspot.com • Luftwaffe A.S – http://luftwaffeas.blogspot.com
• Israeli Air Force IAF EVENTS AND HISTORY SINCE 1948 – http://idf-airforce.blogspot.com
• Oryx Blog – http://spioenkop.blogspot.com • Israel's Good Name – https://israelsgoodname.
wordpress.com • http://www.oocities.org/ • http://vbulletin.degem.net • Wikimedia Commons

LUBLIN 2017

ISBN 978-83-65437-49-5

DISTRIBUTION
Kagero Publishing
ul. Akacjowa 100, os. Borek, Turka, 20-258 Lublin 62, Poland
phone +48 601-602-056, phone/fax +48 81 501-21-05
e-mail: marketing@kagero.pl
www.kagero.pl

Contents

Introduction

The conflict between Israel and the Arab states has been continuing with varying intensity for about 100 years (and in some cases since much earlier times). Undoubtedly, this is the longest armed conflict in the twentieth century and one of the longest conflicts in history.

The dispute over the identity and shape of the territory of Israel is one of the most difficult, and the international community has still not managed to formulate a final opinion on this. After their tragic experiences (especially during the Second World War), the Jewish community decided to create their own state using a "fait accompli". In 1948 there was a war, as a result of which the independent state of Israel was established within the former British Mandate of Palestine.

Arab states recognized this as a humiliation and started a virtually endless war aimed at its elimination. It was (and largely still is) a struggle based mainly on ideological and religious lines. Egypt and Syria had not, in fact, such large material interests in the destruction of the Jewish state, the more so that these wars were associated with huge costs. From a financial point of view, they would benefit a lot more if instead of starting a war, they would have commenced economic cooperation with Israel. In the conditions in the Middle East, this was impossible. The only Arab ethnic group which may have physically gained something from defeating Israel were the Palestinians, but they did not play a major role in the Arab-Israeli wars. The first glimpses of potential cooperation (or at least lack of open war) between Israel and Egypt appeared only as a result of the agreement at Camp David in 1978. After decades of costly wars with Israel, Egypt had to recognize that the defeat and destruction of the country was simply impossible and took the practical decision to discontinue open war. From then on there has been relative peace between Israel and Egypt. The fight against the Jewish state continues to be led by Syria, which significantly reduced its effort after losing the war in Lebanon in the mid-80s, later fighting on the border between Israel and Syria were already far less intense. Currently, Syria is engulfed by civil war, and the focus of its policy is aimed at completely different goals than the struggle against the state of Israel.

Other Arab countries also participated in the wars against Israel (especially Iraq), although the practical cessation of fighting by Egypt also significantly weakened their actions.

Israel, since the beginning of its independence, has acknowledged the great role of the Air Force. The Israeli air force played a leading role in all open wars conducted by the State. Israelis not only tried to equip their armed forces with the most modern aircraft possible, but also drew conclusions concerning the application of the principles and doctrines of the Air Force. The excellent results achieved by Israel's air force confirm that these conclusions were correct.

Arab-Israeli Wars were also a form of fighting between NATO and the Warsaw Pact, because their weapons were tested there. Israel received arms of Western production (initially French, then American), and the Arab states of Egypt and Syria from the beginning were supported by the Soviet Union and its Warsaw Pact allies. The results of these wars demonstrated the superiority of military techniques and philosophy derived from the West. They assumed the primacy of quality and modernity above numbers, which allowed Israel to inflict huge losses on the Arab armies and defend its own independence.

Chapter I of this publication describes the history of the Air Force of Israel and Poland-related topics of countries of the Middle East. Polish themes there were indeed symbolic, but for Polish readers they may be very unfamiliar curiosity. This chapter describes the development of military aviation in Israel since the early aviation organizations in the British Mandate of Palestine in the 30s up to the present day. In addition, this chapter also contains information on Polish exports of aircraft to countries taking part the Israeli-Arab wars as well as co-operation between the Polish air force and Israel, and also other issues related to this.

Chapter II describes the course of aircraft combat during some of the conflicts between Israel and the Arab states. It deals with the Suez Crisis of 1956, the Six Day War of 1967, the Yom Kippur War of 1973 as well as over the Bekaa Valley in Lebanon in 1982. In addition, it describes the probable course of the air war between Israel and Syria at the turn of 20th and 21st centuries. If source materials on the conflicts up to the mid-80s are plentiful, to find references on present struggles from about 2000 is very difficult. They are, in fact too recent events for all information on this topic would have been open to the public. Only specific mentions of the subject get into the media. On this basis we have attempted to present those events.

We have skipped the subject of civil aviation, except for civilian aircraft bearing registration numbers of the British Mandate of Palestine, on which the first Jewish pilots in the late 30s trained.

CHAPTER I

Israeli Air Force and Polish themes in the Middle East Air Forces

1.1. The beginnings of aviation in the British Mandate of Palestine

The first aviation activity in what is now Israel during the interwar period was run by the British armed forces and several civilian air carriers, including the Polish Airline "LOT". The Polish national carrier had limited possibilities of servicing west and east of Europe, so it focused on the north-south direction[1].

One of the greatest achievements of the PLL "LOT" in the interwar period was launching flights from Warsaw to Lydda in Palestine[2] in 1936 with only one stop-over. The route was over 3,000 kilometres via Hungary, Yugoslavia, Greece (with a stopover in Athens), then across the Aegean Sea and the Mediterranean Sea. The longest stretch from Warsaw to Athens amounted to 1,674 km and was carried out at night, lasting 6 hours[3]. Only nine airline companies could afford such an operation, which required modern equipment and highly qualified personnel. The Palestine connection was handled by the most modern aircraft of the "LOT" fleet, including Douglas DC-2. This route was organized in cooperation with the Polish Jewish community. It was not the end of the airline cooperation between Poland and the Jewish community. In Palestine, the RWD-8 RWD 13 and RWD 15 aircraft were also used, some of which took part in the Israeli War of Independence in 1948.

---

[1] Political restrictions on connections of the PLL "LOT" in the interwar period and the organization of connections with Palestine (including cooperation with the Polish Jewish community for this purpose) is described in the memories of the pre-war director of "LOT": W. Makowski, *Cywil w wojsku – wspomnienia z życia i wojen*, Warsaw 2012.

[2] The term Palestine means the League of Nations' mandate of Great Britain in 1920–1947, which is now Israel.

[3] J. Liwiński, *Transport lotniczy w Polsce w okresie międzywojennym*, in: Lotnictwo, Issue 10/2008, p. 76.

It cannot be ruled out that Jewish airmen of Polish descent fought there[4]. Fighting between the Jews and Arabs living in the Palestine mandate had been continuing with varying intensity for a long time. They gained the greatest momentum, how-ever, after World War II, and finally turned into open war. On the Israeli side was a military structure called Haganah[5] which eventually received its air component. In the autumn of 1947 the Jewish community began to prepare for the Arab invasion of Palestine, which would result in the total annexation of the disputed territories, and prevent the emergence of a Jewish state.

Two weeks before the UN voted on Palestine in November 1947 the Haganah had created the first Jewish Air Force (Sherut Avir, Hebrew. שרות תעופה / ריוואה). They consisted initially of 25 light aircraft on loan from the Jewish airlines "Aviron" (including two Polish RWD-8[6] / VQ-PAG and VQ-PAK / two RWD-13 / VQ-PAL and VQ-PAM / and one RWD-15 / VQ-PAE /) and only eleven pilots. They also managed to buy a number of other aircraft, including two Taylorcraft Model C, about 20 Auster A.O.P. light observation aircraft (most officially in private hands), one DH.89 Dragon Rapide (VQ-PAR "Aron") and two DH.82C Tiger Moth (VQ-PAU and VQ-PAV)

---

[4] Later the influx of Jews from Poland to Israel was significant, which also had an impact on the com-position of the Israeli army. Polish soldier serving with the UN mission in Egypt in 1973, B. Świątkiewicz mentions that when having eavesdropped on Israeli aircraft the Polish language could also be heard. See B. Świątkiewicz, *Pod błękitną flagą*, Warsaw, 1975

[5] A training camp of the Haganah (the military organization founded in 1920, the aim of which was self-defense of Jewish settlements in Palestine) was established also in Poland, in Bolków in Lower Silesia in the autumn of 1947. In the larger Polish cities recruiting points arose. Young people of Jewish origin were offered training and a fast trip to the Middle East, where they were to settle down and fight against the Arabs for their new homeland. Anyone who began training signed a declaration that upon arrival in Pal-estine he would join the Haganah. Officially, nothing was mentioned about the Haganah camp in Bolków, but around the town the existence of the camp was no secret, and the relations between the inhabitants of Bolków and trainees were good. Above all, they were watched by the Polish Ministry of Public Security, which approved the list of applicants. Members of the Polish Workers' Party were blackmailed – for them, the condition of consent for the trip was to cooperate with the secret police. They must have committed themselves to denounce their comrades during training and then become intelligence agents in the Middle East. Training in Bolków was run by Haganah envoys, but military instructors who had served in the Red Army and the Polish People's Army were there, too. According to Smolar "they were senior officers, who had no idea about the conditions of the struggle in Israel. The situation changed at a time when Haganah instructors arrived from Munich". The whole training was funded by the American Jewish Joint Distribu-tion Committee. The course lasted 12 hours daily for 10 days. In a course 100–150 volunteers participated. In total, approx. 7,000 men were probably trained. Besides the classic military training and drills, partici-pants learned about Zionism and Palestine. They were all dressed in green US Army surplus uniforms, sent from the USA to Poland. The camp in Bolków was disbanded by the end of 1948. The argument about the need for military training to fight for the independence of Israel, at the moment of the creation of this country ceased to be valid. An additional, or even the most important factor was the political rapproche-ment of Israel and the United States. Source: http://www.sztetl.org.pl/pl/article/bolkow/7,organizacje-i-stowarzyszenia/33378,oboz-szkoleniowy-hagany-w-bolkowie-1947-1948-/

[6] The RWD-8s arrived to Palestine in June 1937 and were used to train pilots for the Haganah. Training continued until September 1939. With the outbreak of World War II, the British banned flights in Palestine. Y. Efrati, *Colors and markings of the Israeli Air Force*, ed. Isra Decals, Israel 2005, p. 5

from Canada. Officially, they were used by the Aero Club of Palestine and in the light of official data were not part of the Sherut Avir. With these aircraft the Jews were trained in 1939 as the first group to own a pilot's travel license. Most likely, they trained on the Polish aircraft RWD-8. These forces were also used to carry out reconnaissance and air supply for cut-off Jewish communities.

The secret organization Haganah (Defense) was founded in 1920 by Vladimir Jabotinsky (Żabotyński)[7]. It was established to defend the Jewish population from attacks by Arab militias, whose attacks had intensified in 1936–1939. The main tasks of the Haganah were the acquisition of weapons, training fighters, and intelligence. During World War II, the Haganah supported the British and had its agents in many countries. This organization also created its air force in 1947. Initially, the air force of the later state of Israel was based on complete improvisation. The first bases of the newly formed Sherut Avir were mainly the Aero Club of Palestine and the "Aviron" company – both were under the total control of the Haganah. A network of relatively well-prepared airstrips was also available (which had been created by the Jews in Palestine since 1937) and about 2,500 people (of both genders), many of whom had experience of service with the Allied armies and air forces[8]. Perhaps some of them had served in the Polish Air Force in the West. A number of pilots of Jewish origin was surely also present in the Polish aviation regiments in the USSR[9].

The first chief of staff Sherut Avir was Aharon Remez. In 1948 Sherut Avir acquired the first of three Beechcraft Bonanza aircraft bought by Boris Senior – a former British military pilot from South Africa. Officially, the aircraft was flying on a tourist trip to Europe, but landed in the Negev desert, where bomb racks were installed. Soon after Sherut Avir acquired heavy transport planes. American Jewish A. W. Shwimmer (pilot and flight engineer) bought in the US ten Curtiss C-46 Commando aircraft and three Lockheed L-049 Constellation from USAF storage. They were then registered in Panama. They were used, among others, to bring weapons to Israel. For example, L-049 with the Panamanian registration number RX-121 when flying through Europe, was involved in the transport of weapons from Czechoslovakia.

In addition, during the seven months of Sherut Avir's existence (from November 1947 to May 1948) the aviation of Haganah received many other aircraft. In March of 1948, Haganah commandeered a Fairchild F24R (UC-61) belonging to an Egyptian drugs smuggler. In May, they purchased three DH.89 Dragon Rapide in the UK. An RC-3 Seabee float plane and three C-47s were purchased. Also four Avro

---

[7]   Organization of the Haganah was described in detail in: P. Przymusiała, *Haganah*, "Aero Technika Lotnicza", Issues 6 and 7/1990. On the basis of this article we describe the early years of aviation in Israel.

[8]   R. Ball, *The Israeli Air Force Part One 1948 to 1967*, Guideline Publications, UK, 2000, p. 3.

[9]   A story of one of the Polish Jewish airmen serving with the Polish Air Force in the USSR is described in: W. Zmyślony, *Grób chorążego Brocha*, "Militaria XXW", Issue No. 3 (48) / 2012.

Anson training aircraft were bought, but these were interned in Greece. In Israel, there were also a number of Lockheed Hudson Mk III and Lodestar aircraft. On April 13 the only RWD-15 was burned at the Lod Airport as a result of sabotage.

The first combat mission of the Israeli Air Force was the flight of Polish production RWD-13 piloted by Pinachas Ben-Porat which took place on 17th December 1947. He was to carry a doctor to Beth-Eshel in the Negev desert and then fly to the vicinity Nvatim, where he was to collect two wounded and evacuate them to the north. When Ben-Porat had come to Beth-Eshel he learned that Nvatim was being invaded by about 200 Arabs. Ben-Porat asked for a machine gun and several grenades. Then he removed the door of the RWD-13 and tied a Bren gun to a seat. He took off with a volunteer gunner. A few minutes later, the aircraft attacked the Arab forces at Nvatim, forcing them to withdraw[10].

After it had been reported that the Israelis used an armed aircraft in combat, the British authorities announced that any Israeli plane carrying weapons could be shot down without warning. Pilot Pinachas Ben-Porat was killed on 27 July 1955 when his L-049 Constellation (4X-AKC) belonging to the "El-Al" airline was shot down by Bulgarian MiG-15 fighters over Bulgaria.

1.2. Air combat in 1948

Even before athe final collapse of the British rule over Palestine, there were the first fights with the use of aviation of both sides. At midnight on 14th/15th May 1948 the newborn state of Israel was attacked from all sides by the forces of the Arab countries: Egyptian, Syrian, Lebanese and Jordanian, as well as by smaller Iraqi, Sudanese, Saudi and Moroccan contingents. Most combat sorties were carried by Royal Egyptian Air Force (REAF) which possessed about 40 Spitfire Mk.VC/Trop and Mk.IX fighters, 25 DC-3 Dakotas capable of carrying bombs, 5 Hawker Furys, 20 Westland Lysanders and about 30 other types.

In the morning of May 15th an Egyptian Spitfire LF Mk.IX attacked a power station near the Israeli base of Lod. It was damaged by fire from the ground and force landed nearby. After it had been refurbished it was incorporated into the Israeli Air Force. But Sherut Avir needed more fighters.

In the 40s Israel maintained good relations with Communist states. The Soviet Union had hoped that the Jewish state could be a good bulwark of socialism in the Middle East, especially when the Arab countries kept numerous contacts with Britain and France. Therefore in 1948 talks with Czechoslovakia on the supply of Avia S-199 fighters began. It was a local version of the German Messershmitt Bf-109G

---

[10] S. Aloni, *Arab-Israeli Air Wars...*, p. 7 and http://www.jewishvirtuallibrary.org/jsource/Society_&_Culture/rwd13.html

with a Junkers Jumo 211F (1,190 hp) engine from the Heinkel He-111 bomber. After $1.8 million had been paid, the Czechs delivered the planes to the airport at Žatec, which was a base for the Haganah in Czechoslovakia. These fighters were brought to Israel on transport C-54 planes which bore civilian markings. Unfortunately, in contrast to its German original, the S-199 proved to be a very unsuccessful fighter. The Jumo 211F engine was intended for bombers and did not matche the flight characteristics of fighter. The S-199 tended to tilt significantly on the wing during takeoff or landing. Then the plane hit the ground, capsized and ended up in flames. The canopy tilted to one side which hindered or prevented the evacuation of the pilot. In one case the pilot of an overturned Avia was released only after a day of struggling with a jammed canopy. The S-199 achieved insufficient speed for a fighter of the late 40s – 547 km/h and for this reason it was nicknamed "the mule". There were no other fighters, however, in Israel thus the "mules" had to be used in combat. They were manned mainly by the volunteers from the US, Canada, Great Britain and South Africa, who agreed to serve in the Air Force of Israel for symbolic pay. They were not only Jews. They were attracted by the possibility of fighting and flying. P. Przymusiała says that some of them made their living from stealing cars in Palestine[11]. Some of the volunteers already had an impressive service record. For example, Chalmers H. Goodlin (the test pilot of an engineless version of the Bell X-1), Boni Senior (South African air forces ace), Paul Homeski (formerly served with the Free French Air Force), Ezer Weizman[12] (RAF), Lee Sinclair (former RAF wing commander) "Buck" Feldman (USAF), Caesar Dangott (USAF), John H. McElroy (former RCAF squadron commander) and probably the most famous of them, the Canadian George F. Screwball ("Skewball") Beurling, who was an RAF pilot on Malta and shot down 27 Italian and German aircraft. He volunteered to pass on to Israel one of three Noorduyn C-64A Norseman transport aircraft purchased from the USAF (allegedly for Belgian Line air). They took on a cargo of medicines at Rome. On May 20th, shortly after takeoff from Urbe, an engine of the aircraft piloted by Beurlinga, which had been damaged by saboteurs, stopped working and the overburdened plane crashed (the pilot died). The type of plane which was so unfortunate for Beurling, became a very valuable asset for Israel. Of the twenty C-46As which had been purchased, 17 aircraft reached Israel (as well as the one

---

[11]   P. Przymusiała, *Haganah...*, Part. 1, p. 35.

[12]   E. Weizman (1924–2005) was the only Palestinian citizen who fought in the Battle of Britain in 1940. He served a number of military and political functions in Israel. In 1958–1966 he headed the Air Force, and from 1967 was deputy chief of the General Staff. As coordinator of aviation he played an important role in the Six Day War against the Arab states. He was president of Israel in 1993–2000. http://www.jewishvirtuallibrary.org/jsource/ww2/sugar4.html

lost in Rome, due to navigational errors two other aircraft landed at Ghaza – at the Egyptian REAF airbase)[13].

At that time, Tel Aviv and a number of other Israeli towns were attacked by the Egyptian air force. On 15 May Arab bombs destroyed an RWD-8 and a Seabee. In the following days during sorties Israel lost both Tiger Moths and several Austers which were used as assault planes(!). The tasks of the Egyptian bombers was mainly fulfilled by ad hoc modified DC-3 Dakotas. The Egyptians used their Spitfires and Lysanders in the role of ground support aircraft. They managed to eliminate about half of the Israel's aviation fleet, but almost all of these aircraft with the exception of four were repairable. On 22 May the Ramat David airfield near Haifa was bombed by an Egyptian Spitfire, which destroyed several British aircraft, including two Sptifires RF 18 of 32 Squadron RAF and a Dakota, having mistaken them for Israeli aircraft. Two hours later, there was another Egyptian raid on this airbase. Another Dakota was destroyed and seven other British aircraft damaged. This time British fighters managed to shoot down two Egyptian Spitfires, and a third was shot down by AA defenses. The next day, Egypt apologized to Britain for a „regrettable error in navigation".

The Israelis drew very important conclusions from this incident. First, Egypt had poor intelligence, which could not determine which of the British bases had already been taken over by Israel. Secondly, more raids on Israeli airfields were only a matter of time, so Israel needed more fighters.

The first four Avia S-199s which had been brought to Israel were incorporated into the Tel Aviv, Herzlia and Sde Dov airfields defense flights. In late May, Egyptian troops under Colonel Neguiba were only 40 km from Tel Aviv. On 29 May the S-199s were first used in combat and attacked the Egyptian armoured column. Material losses were small, but the Egyptians were shocked. The Avias showed further defects. During firing, maintaining the target in the viewfinder was impossible due to the vibrations caused by shooting. In addition, firing the guns placed above the engine could result in shooting off the propeller blades because of faulty synchronizers. The wireless sets in the S-199s also often did not work. P. Przymusiała claims[14]: Long afterwards one of the former pilots stated that this was unquestionably the worst aircraft in the world built after 1945. He had the impression that it was constructed by saboteurs.

Soon Sherut Avir ceased to be merely "air service" and was transformed into Chel Ha Avir, or IAF – Israeli Air Force, and on May 30 the Haganah came out of the "underground" havingfbecome the official organization – the Tsvah Haganah le Yisrael, IDF – Israeli Defence Force.

---

[13] P. Przymusiała, *Haganah…*, Part. 1, p. 35.
[14] *Ibidem*, p. 40.

On 1 June, Israeli aircraft bombed Amman. In retaliation, the Arabs made several similar raids. On 3 June, two Egyptian Dakotas escorted by four Spitfires flew in from the sea over Tel Aviv. By then a pair of S-199s was on routine combat air patrol. One of them piloted by former RAF pilot Modi Alon, attacked the Egyptians out of the sun. The Egyptian fighters fled after having noticed the attack, and Alon shot down one Dakota and the other was seriously damaged (it then crash landed in Egypt).

On 4 June the Egyptian navy approached Tel Aviv. It was attacked by an Israeli formation composed of a Dragon Rapide, a Fairchild F24R, a Bonanza and other light aircraft. The bombs forced the Egyptian ships to retreat. The Egyptians, however, shot down an Israeli F24. On 27 June an Egyptian Sea Fury shot down an Israeli Auster.

Upon receipt of four C-47s Israel also transformed them into bombers. They carried out a series of raids on cities in the West Bank, and on 11 June bombed Damascus. On the same day at 1000 hrs a ceasefire between the warring parties began. This time was used to regenerate, reinforce and redeploy troops. Israel basically already had no reserves in manpower, all those capable of bearing arms had fought against Syrian, Iraqi and Lebanese troops in the north, the Saudi Arab Legion in Jerusalem and the Egyptian army in the Negev desert. In addition, several towns in the territory allocated to Israel by the UN resolution were still controlled by the Palestinian police. Israeli troops finally stopped the Arab onslaught having lost a third of its territory. But it was keeping the enemy at bay, without the possibility of making any further movements[15].

The lull in the fighting was used to further arms purchases. Until 11 June, 11 S-199s of 25 which had been acquired were received. At the same time the Israeli authorities negotiated the purchase of 50 Spitfire Mk.IX and Mk.XVI fighters from Czechoslovakia and on the subsequent provision of airfields in Europe. It managed to get permission to use and operate from airfields on Corsica in France and Podgorica in Yugoslavia. In the meantime, the air traffic of strange aircraft with Panamanian registration numbers started to draw attention of the Americans and the British.

In the UK, the Haganah agents bought six Bristol Beaufighters registrations G-AJMB and G-AJMG. Officially they purchased them for a film dedicated to New Zealand airmen. There was even a fictional film crew. Israel eventually received four Beaufighters.

Military operations began again on 9 July. Israel then for the first time used the air force to support mechanized infantry attacking the towns of Lydda and Ramlech. The next day the action to take back the town of Michmar from the Syrians began, where Israeli troops had air support. The Syrians used their Harvards as ground attack aircraft, which inflicted heavy losses on the Israeli troops. Only when one of

---

[15] *Ibidem.*

them was shot down (probably by an S-199) the Syrian Harvards withdrew. Israel lost one S-199 then while it tried to intercept another Harvard.

Despite the embargo, Israel still managed to acquire more aviation equipment. The aforementioned A. W. Schwimmer was able to buy four Boeing B-17G bombers in the US. However, they were stripped of military equipment, including wireless sets and navigation devices. In one of them the radio compass was missing. Officially they were sold as transport aircraft to South America. Although the condition of the aircraft was poor, once their ability to fly had been confirmed, it was decided to take off from Miami on a flight via Greenland to Czechoslovakia. Three of them arrived there, and Czech and Israeli technicians began to restore their combat and navigation equipment. However, they managed to get only one bomb sight, which had been removed from the wreckage of a German bomber.

On 8 July the ceasefire came to an end and the Israeli B-17s with bombs loaded in Czechoslovakia flying on the way to Israel, made a raid on targets in Sinai as well as on Cairo. Their crews did not have proper navigational documentation, only maps torn from encyclopedias. The ADF radio compasses, set on the RAF station at Fayid. All three B-17 reached Israel. Material losses on the Egyptian side were symbolic, but induced shock in the enemy. As a result of these raids the Egyptians and Syrians withdrew part of their fighter strength from the frontline and moved them to guard strategic facilities within both countries.

At that time, there were several dogfights between the Israeli S-199 and Egyptian aircraft. One Egyptian Spitfire Mk.V was shot down for the loss of two two S-199s.

On 19 July another ceasefire was signed, but fighting still continued with less intensity. Israel would then get some American P-51D Mustangs and C-54 transport aircraft, as well as a reconnaissance Mosquito PR.XVI.

In the last days of July 1948 the Ministry of Defence of Czechoslovakia informed the Israeli authorities that, due to pressure from the US ambassador, maintaining the base at Žatec was not any longer possible and within 14 days Israel should leave it and evacuate its personnel – especially the US citizens. Although the Czechs assured these measures were of only temporary nature, the Israelis started to evacuate all the collected materials, including spare parts and ammunition for the S-199s and Spitfires. Within a week 40t of equipment including 26 tonnes of bombs was taken away. Nevertheless, the Czechoslovak authorities in need of hard currency continued to give support to Israel, although it was much smaller. In September, under the codename "Balalaika" delivery of the former Czechoslovak Spitfires began with a stopover in Titograd. The transport aircraft (usually C-54s) also took part in the operation, guiding the Spitfires. Flight route was as much as possible and regularly monitored by Israeli ships, and in Haifa there was a DC-3 ready to fly with rescue equipment[16].

---

[16]   P. Przymusiała, *Haganah...*, Part. 2, p. 31.

Later, the Israeli Air Force supported the ground troops with Spitfires, Beaufighters, B-17s, C-46s and C-47s. The last stage of the conflict is described P. Przymusiała[17]: November 11, 1948. The UN Security Council urged the warring parties to cease firing and start talks, but the Egyptian side refused to take part in them, and Israel recognized that success in battle did not force it to make such moves. <u>The Chel Ha'Avir by then had 113 aircraft, including 70 fighters and bombers</u> (underline – J. M.). The REAF was experiencing a severe crisis, some of their aircraft would have been scrapped in order to obtain spare parts for others. Thus, Egyptian opposition declined to such an extent that the Israeli Air Force operated almost undisturbed. On 23 December operation "Horav" was launched, the biggest and final attempt to oust Egyptian forces from the lands of Israel, and inflict losses to prevent any aggression in the future. Despite heavy losses Gaza was seized, on 28 December Abu-Agheila was captured and the Bir Hasa-on and El Hama air bases were attacked. On 30 December a column of Israeli troops occupied the aifield at El Arish and stopped at the gates of the town of the same name, located 7 km north of the airfield. Because of a note from the British government, referring to the 20-year-old Anglo-Egyptian friendship and a warning by the US government which demanded withdrawal of Israeli troops from the territory of Egypt, the authorities in Tel Aviv took into account the possibility of British intervention. However, after fierce fighting, on 6 January 1949 the remnants of Egyptian forces in the Gaza Strip were cut off from outside help and on the same day Cairo declared a readiness for peace and cessation of hostilities. The truce came into life at midnight 6/7 January 1949.

1.3. Subsequent development of the Israeli Air Force

From 1958 Israel started to receive the first deliveries of the French Super Mystere and Mirage IV IIIC[18] fighters, Vautour II ground attack aircraft, Fouga CM.170 Magister training jets and Super Frelon heavy helicopters. On 27 September 1962, US President John F. Kennedy agreed to sell to Israel 48 A-4H Skyhawk ground attack aircraft as well as Sikorsky H-34 and Bell 205 helicopters (delivered only after the 1967 war).

In 1966 and 1967 in response to the terrorist attacks and artillery bombardments Israeli aircraft repeatedly carried out retaliatory raids on the Syrian positions on the Golan Heights. On 7 April 1967 there was an air battle, during which six Syrian

---

[17] *Ibidem.*

[18] With the Mirage III fighters, Israel received its first air-to-air missiles, the Matra R.530 – as demonstrated by the fact they are only capable to destroy less maneuverable targets like the Tu-16 or Il-28 bombers, to hit a fighter would be a miracle (there was only one case – an Egyptian MiG-19 was shot down).

MiG-21s were shot down. After the battle, Israeli fighter jets performed a demonstration flight over Damascus – the capital of Syria.

In later years, Israeli Air Force took part in battles as a part of a series of conflicts, which will be described in detail in the next chapter. This applies to such conflicts as the the Suez crisis (1956), Six-Day War (1967), the Yom Kippur War (1973), fighting over the valley of Bekaa in Lebanon (1982) and possible air combats against the Syrians in the first years of 21st century. In all these conflicts a huge role was played by Israeli Air Force, which although far less numerous than the air forces of the Arab countries, have proven to be much more efficient. The Israeli Air Force almost every time quickly made a decisive blow to the Arab countries that saved the Jewish state when it was facing aggression and collapse.

Among the most important events in the history of the Air Force of Israel are among others[19]:

On 20 December 1976 the United States began delivery of F-15 Eagles, which as early as 1979 were used in combat – in March they shot down a Syrian MiG-21 over Lebanon, and by mid-1982 the Israeli Eagles' balance of clashes with Syrian fighters officially was already 15:0. In addition, the F-15s were used in the role of ground attack machines, on 9 June destroyed 19 Syrian anti-aircraft missile launcher sites in the Bekaa Valley. A week after the operation, Israeli F-15s shot down about 45 Syrian fighters (mostly MiG-21s and MiG-23s). Another significant success of these aircraft was the downing of an unmarked MiG-25[20]. In 1993 it was decided to purchase 25 F-15I Raam, a variant of the two-seat F-15E Strike Eagle developed according to Israeli demands.

In March of 1978 the first multi-purpose F-16 Fighting Falcons were purchased, which later became one of the pillars of the Israeli strike force. Interestingly, the first batch of Israeli F-16 was initially built for Iran. In 1979 Israel took over the entire Iranian order which was cancelled, i.e. 75 F-16 fighters. Iran after the Islamic Revolution became an enemy of the United States and further arms supplies to this country stopped. At the same time the US granted large financial support for the construction of modern air force bases in the Negev desert. This was a reward from the US administration for the Camp David peace agreement with Egypt which had been signed two years earlier, which ultimately ended open war with that country. The combat debut of the F-16s (nicknamed "Netz", Falcon) was shooting down two Syrian Mi-8 helicopters over the Lebanese town of Zahle, on 28 April 1981. A new batch of F-16,

---

[19] See also: P. Cebulok, *Izraelskie Siły Powietrzne – historia i teraźniejszość*, "Nowa Technika Wojskowa", Issue No. 11/1995 and M. Pospisil, M. J. Stolár, *Siły Powietrzne i Kosmiczne Sił Obronnych Izraela*, "Lotnictwo", Issue No. 1/2010

[20] It is difficult to say whether the MiG-25 was indeed unmarked or Israeli pilots could not see the Syrian markings, which for this type of aircraft were very small.

part of which included not only the F-16A/Bs but also the F-16C/D was delivered from 1985. Once the order had been completed, the IAF had in stock 57 F-16As, 7 F-16Bs, 59 F-16Cs and 26 F-16Ds. An order for a further sixty F-16C/D Block 40 aircraft was the result of cancellation of its the own aircraft programme of a similar class machine called the IAI Lavi. In Israel an extensive modernization of the electronic equipment of the F-16s was carried out, under which the fairing under the vertical stabilizer was extended (detailed information about the type of equipment located there is classified).

At the 1991 balance in air combat of the Israeli F-16s, according to official data was 44: 0. Then the specialist Israeli two-seat variant F-16I was introduced intended not to train, but to perform very complex tasks in combat for which a single pilot could be saddled with too many responsibilities. In 2001 it was agreed that America would provide 102 F-16Is at a cost of $4.5 billion. The first unit equipped with these machines was combat ready in 2004. Today, Israel is the second largest user of the F-16s after the US (in 2008 there was a total of 108 F-16A/Bs, 136 F-16C/Ds and 80 F-16Is).

On 7 June 1981 the Israeli Air Force carried out operation "Opera", under which it bombed the Iraqi nuclear reactor. Eight F-16 aircraft armed with Mark 84 bombs and escorted by six F-15s flew over the territory of Jordan and Saudi Arabia, and then bombed the Osirak reactor and returned to base without encountering Iraqi aircraft or incurring losses from fire from the ground. This attack, though successful from the perspective of the military, sparked a big diplomatic scandal and for a while deliveries of American military equipment to Israel were suspended – but all the aircraft ordered arrived in 1982. Generally, the leaders of many countries were aware that the acquisition by Iraq under Saddam Hussein of the ability to build a nuclear bomb would constitute a major threat not only for Israel but also for the whole civilized world.

Since the first Lebanon War in 1982–1985, Israeli Air Force did not participate in any open armed conflict until the second Lebanon war waged in the summer of 2006 in which the IAF played a leading role. Israeli operations in Lebanon began from raids carried out by the IAF, the targets included the main road of the country, the Beirut-Damascus route (with aircraft), as well as the civilian-military international airport named after Rafik Hariri (using helicopters). In this conflict there was no air combat as the Arab guerrilla groups against which Israel fought did not have any aviation. Presumably, however, there was sporadic fighting with the Syrian air forces over Lebanon in 2001–2002 (see next chapter).

Shortly after midnight on 6 September 2007, the Israeli Air Force carried out an air strike on an alleged Syrian nuclear reactor (operation "Orchard")[21], which was

---

[21] See: Officials say Israel raid on Syria triggered by arms fears, Reuters 2007 http://uk.reuters. com/article/uk-syria-israel-targets-idUKSCH23352020070912; and Bar-Zochar M., Mishal N., *Mossad. The great operations*, Harper Collins Publ. 2012, ISBN 978-83-7510-898-9.

in muhafaza (province) Deir el-Zor. According to US intelligence, built with Syrian-North Korean co-operation, this nuclear installation was used for military purposes.

Syria, of course, denied these accusations[22]. A preliminary report of the International Atomic Energy Agency (IAEA) acknowledged that there was no clear evidence that there were ongoing works of a military nature. Later, however, some traces of processed uranium were found. There were, nevertheless, voices that such evidence was insufficient to prove the existence of a reactor. It was recognized, however, that building a nuclear reactor is possible, and possession of nuclear technology by Syria would be too great a threat to Israel (and not only that). It was decided to destroy it. According to "The Sunday Times" members of the Israeli special forces Sayeret Matkal secretly infiltrated near the Syrian nuclear installation before the attack, to take samples of nuclear materials and deliver them to Israel. Analysis of the samples acquired indicated their origin from North Korea. The press also reported that after the results had been made known the United States supposedly gave Israel permission to conduct the strike[23]. The United States, however, denied any involvement in the preparation or approval of the attack, confirming only that they had been informed of the operation in advance[24].

The strike group consisted of F-15Is, F-16Is Sufa and one recce aircraft[25]. In total, in the first phase of the operation eight aircraft were involved, of which at least four, having maintained low height, entered the airspace of Syria[26]. The fighters were armed with AGM-65 Maverick missiles and bombs weighing 227 kg each. The operation was also assisted by a team from the elite Israeli commando unit Sayeret Matkal. The commandos arrived at the place on the day before the attack to mark targets with laser beams during the strike[27].

Interestingly, during attacks on ground targets Israel still relies in a large extent on classic free falling unguided bombs, supported by highly precise sighting equipment in the aircraft. The main performers of these ground strikes are two seater F-16Is.

Great importance is being attached to the ability to perform tactical airborne landings in the rear of the enemy – for this very purpose a fleet of heavy and medium transport aircraft and helicopters is maintained. Despite the small size of the country, Israel maintains a fleet of flying tankers, too. This reflects the political doctrine of assuming the defense of the interests of Israel and Jews around the world.

---

[22] US accuses Syria of building secret reactor with N Korea's help, 2008 http://web.archive.org/web/20110520132008/http://afp.google.com/article/ALeqM5jWIBgbzyBkHnJzQeMi80gXfjX0-Q
[23] Snatched: Israeli commandos ,nuclear' raid, in: "The Sunday Times", 23.10.2007.
[24] P. Hess, White House says Syria ,must come clean' about nuclear work, in: "The Associated Press", 25.04.2008.
[25] Israelis blew apart Syrian nuclear cache, in "The Sunday Times", 16.09.2007.
[26] S. M. Hersh, A Strike in the Dark, in "The New Yorker", 11.02.2008.
[27] P. Beaumont, Was Israeli raid a dry run for attack on Iran?, in "The Observer", 16.09.2007.

Despite having a relatively well-developed aerospace industry Israel currently does not produce or does not develop any of its own design of manned combat aircraft (the programme of its own IAI Lavi[28] fighter aircraft was dropped).

Israeli industry, however, is able to carry out deep modernization of aviation and combat equipment. These capabilities are widely used by the IAF in upgrading the F-16 aircraft and the production of their sub-assemblies[29].

The only Israeli fighter jet which went into production was the IAI Kfir/Nesher of 1971[30]. It was a local variant of the French Mirage III, and the background to its development is quite sensational. Specialists of the Israeli Air Force believed that the electronics of the Mirage III were too sophisticated for the weather conditions of the Middle East.

A simpler and cheaper version of the aircraft was ordered from Dassault Aviation. The result of this work was the Mirage V[31], of which Israel ordered 50 aircraft under the designation Mirage 5J. After the Six-Day War in 1967, France imposed an official embargo on Israel. Deliveries of the Mirage V fighter jet to this country stopped, despite the fact that Israel had paid the down payment and several installments. Having anticipated this possibility Israel started research into the development of the Mirage IIIC to upgrade it to the multi-purpose aircraft level, i.e. a fighter, interceptor and ground attack plane. The Israeli Air Force needed in a short time to replenish losses which had been suffered until 1967 (in 1962–1967 Israel lost a total of 20% of the original number of the fighter aircraft), all the more as Egyptian aviation began to recover very quickly thanks to supplies from the Soviet Union – a month after the Six Day war, Egypt had about 200 fighters, including the latest MiG-21 and Su-7. IAI responded immediately with a project similar to the Mirage 5, the Nesher, which was based on the airframe of the Mirage IIIC. Technical details were obtained through the work of Mossad spies.

---

[28] The Israeli aircraft company IAI (Israel Aircraft Industries) was founded in 1953 as Bedek Aviation Company. From the beginning, the main task of the plant was to support the Israeli Defense Forces. In the next decade the IAI single-handedly built under license from the French the Fouga CM.170 Magister training aircraft (Israeli codename IAI Snunit). At the end of the 60's it produced the first entirely domestic design of multi-purpose aircraft, the short take-off and landing (STOL) IAI Arava. Another machine was a civilian plane IAI Westwind which was a modified version of the American Aero Commander 1121 Jet Commander. On the basis of the Westwind marine patrol aircraft the IAI Sea Scan was built. In September 1969 the IAI Nesher flew for the first time which was a modified version of the French Mirage fighter. At the end of the 60's the Israeli aerospace industry employed about 7,000 people.

[29] It is worth noting that a number of components and equipment of Polish F-16C/D Hawks have also been produced in Israel. "Skrzydlata Polska" in Issue No. 03/2007 says that parts manufactured in Israel for Polish F-16s include among others: reconnaissance pods, horizontal stabilizers, rudders, wings and elements of on-board equipment. The conformal tanks (CFT) are also made in Israel.

[30] See R. Kwas, M. Gołembiewski, *IAI Kfir*, AJ-Press, Gdańsk, 1996.

[31] One Mirage V BA (license No. BA 21) obtained from Belgium in the 90s is displayed at the Air Forces Museum in Dęblin, Poland. The second Mirage V BA (No. BA 03) is located in the Polish Aviation Museum, Kraków, Poland.

Later, there were reports that France, which took over the already built Mirage 5J for Israel as the Mirage 5F in 1972 agreed to deliver to Israel in secrecy kits to assemble the aircraft in place by IAI. "El Al" airline planes supposedly helped in their transportation, having landed in Merignac. The documents described them as spare parts for Mirage IIIs. Under this undisclosed license Israel received the full technical documentation, devoid however, of plans of key components, especially the SNECMA Atar 09c-3 engines with 42 kN thrust, which were delivered complete. Israel illegally bought, however, the plans of these engines from a citizen of Switzerland, where the Mirage IIIs were produced under license. A version of the act of stealing the entire documentation of the Mirage (not only the engine itself) would be created to explain the presence of aircraft embargoed in Israel, the French benefited from it by selling about 200 Mirage 5 to Arab countries (including Libya and Egypt). At that time, the Israeli company Elta prepared to license the production of the Thomson CSF Aida II radar, which was to be installed in the Mirage 5Js. Radar was supposed to replace the more complex radar station Cyrano 1A of the Mirage IIICJ. Israeli industry had for some time been producing the DEFA 552 cannon (30 mm) and a number of parts for the Mirage III.

IAI built 61 of these aircraft, some of which were exported under the designation Dagger to Argentina. The last Nesher in Israeli service was withdrawn in 1980. These aircraft were replaced by an improved version called IAI Kfir, which was produced thanks to the favour of the United States which supplied the American General Electric J-79 engine. They were also used by the US Air Force (USAF) as the F-21 Dagger, and served in the "Aggressors" units (playing the role of enemy fighters during exercises).

IAI also takes part in the modernization of existing military aircraft, one of which was the project MiG-21-2000 Lancer[32]. In cooperation with Elbit, the Romanians modernized their MiG-21 fighter jets to the Lancer standard. Also, Israel modernized MiG-21 aircraft for Cambodia, Laos and Ethiopia. IAI offered a similar service to Poland, but it never materialized.

Due to the high importance attached to protecting the lives of soldiers (Israel is a relatively low populated country), the Israeli Air Force is to the great extent equipped with unmanned aircraft, both for reconnaissance and combat of American and local manufacture.

At the beginning of the 70s the first Israeli unmanned aircraft (Unmanned Aerial Vehicle – UAV) IAI Scout was produced, which together with other similar ma-

---

[32] More on the Israeli variants of MiG-21 in: Y. Gordon B. Gunston, *MiG-21 Fishbed*, Aerofax, Leicester, UK, 1996, p. 87–91 and Y. Gordon, K. Dexter, D. Komissarov, *Mikoyan MiG-21*, Midland, UK, 2008, p. 481, 603–604; *Migiem w XXI wiek*, in: "Skrzydlata Polska", Issue No. 01/1993 and J. Gruszczyński, T. Mikutel, E. F. Rybak, C. Piotrowski, R. Gretzyngier, *MiG-21*, in: "Przegląd Konstrukcji Lotniczych" No. 25, Altair, Warsaw 1995, p. 11.

chine called Mastiff designed in Tadiran Electronic Industries (later incorporated into IAI) became the first of this type of aircraft in Israeli armed forces. Continuing development and refinement resulted in the development of UAVs produced more machines: IAI Searcher, IAI Heron and IAI Harpy. The latter has a warhead designed to destroy any radar stations detected. Harpy's development is another armed UAV – IAI Harop. The IAI UAVs are being used by many armies of the world, the company's work has been recognized and used in the design and construction of the Swiss unmanned aircraft ADS 95 Ranger and American UAVs RQ-2 Pioneer and the RQ-5 Hunter. The Second Lebanon War, which took place in 2006, contributed a shift in focus also in the development of small unmanned aerial machines (take-off weight of about 50–250 kg) of the IAI "I-view" family, which can be used below brigade level.

IAI participated in the design and construction of the Israeli spy satellites Ofeq and the Shavit rocket, which carried the satellites into orbit. Besides Ofeq, IAI also built the TecSAR satellite (also known as TechSAR or Polaris). It is a new spy satellite, launched into orbit on 21 January 2008, which was equipped by ELTA Systems LTD with a synthetic aperture radar. IAI also built the series of Eros satellites for civilian projects, used for earth observation and the Amos telecommunications satellites.

These were not the first experiences of IAI as far as rocket technology is concerned. Already in 1968 the Israelis had conducted tests of the ballistic missile Jericho-1, which was a development version of the French design Dassault MD-600. Probably around 100 Jericho-1 missiles were built. Presumably it could carry a warhead weighing 500 kg, including conventional, chemical and nuclear variants. The Jericho-1 entered service in 1973. This new weapon made possible to hit targets located at a distance of 750 km. The missile was adapted to carry tactical nuclear warheads[33]. The Jericho-1 missiles and their improved version, the Jericho-2 are able to reach cities such as Damascus, Aleppo and Cairo.

1.4. Tests of MiGs in Israel

MiG (Mikoyan Gurevich) aircraft were the backbone of the air forces of Arab countries in the second half of the twentieth century, and in some of these countries remain in use to date (e.g. Syria). It is therefore obvious that the Israeli services tried to get as much information about the aircraft and the best way was to obtain such aircraft and test them in situ. The first aircraft of this type in Israel was an Egyptian MiG-15, captured on 31 October 1956. It was hit in the air and landed in a damaged condition.

---

[33] http://www.globalsecurity.org/wmd/world/israel/jericho-1.htm

On 12 August 1968 two Syrian MiG-17Fs landed by mistake at the Israeli airbase at Betzet[34]. Thereafter, at least one received the Israeli markings and was used in tests in the air (also in the USA).

The most spectacular circumstances, however, accompanied the capture by Israel of a supersonic MiG-21. This was the so-called operation "Diamond" (Hebrew: מִבְצָע יַהֲלוֹם, Mivtza Yahalom) carried out by Mossad[35]. Its aim was to obtain a MiG-21, then the most modern fighter in the arsenal of the Arab states. The operation began in mid-1963 and was completed on 16 August 1966 when an Iraqi pilot of Assyrian origin (and a Christian) Capt. Munir Rodfa landed his MiG-21F13 No. 534 at the base Hatzor in Israel.

It had no missiles but it did have a loaded cannon. Meanwhile, Mossad evacuated the pilot's family from Iraq to Israel. Later this element of the operation proved to be the most difficult. It turned out, in fact, that the organization of a new life in a country with a completely different culture was almost impossible. F. Fetke and K. Izak[36] describe it in a following way: *Mossad revealed to the Americans the secrets of its construction in exchange for the transfer of information on the new Soviet S-75 anti-aircraft missile. Examination of the technological characteristics of MiG-21 proved to be very helpful for the Israeli Air Force and played an important role in preparation for the confrontation with the Arab MiGs, which occurred in June 1967 during the Six Day War. Mossad helped Munir Redfa and his family to settle in Israel, but the Iraqis could not acclimatize. Therefore a trip under a new identity was organized for them to Western Europe. But even here, far from home and family, surrounded by Israeli agents they felt alone. A high rinking Mossad officer formulated an important thesis that building a new life for the culturally alienated agent outside his own country was almost impossible. This conclusion is still quite valid and should be taken into account by the Polish services when organizing the trip and stay in our country for the Afghan co-operators of the Polish Military Contingent before its withdrawal from Afghanistan.*

That MiG-21F13 would soon be given a set of Israeli markings and the number 007 (a reference to the way in which it captured). Tests were conducted by Israeli test pilot Colonel Danny Shapira. It was compared with Israeli fighter jets. Overall, the machine performed well, but its shortcomings were noticed such as poor visibility from the canopy and poor maneuverability at low speeds at low altitude. For example, it turned out that a MiG-21F13 pilot could not see the enemy attacking

---

[34] On the Internet one can find information that these MiGs were of Polish manufacture i.e. Lim-5s.

[35] Bar-Zochar M., Mishal N., *Mossad. The great operations*, Harper Collins Publ. 2012, ISBN 978-83-7510-898-9.

[36] F. Fetke, K. Izak, review of the Bar-Zochar M., Mishal N., *Mossad. The great operations*, Harper Collins Publ. 2012, ISBN 978-83-7510-898-9.

from the rear at an angle less[37] than 30 degrees. Once it had been tested in Israel, the plane was tested in the US and then returned. Currently, it is in the museum in Hatzerim. In addition to the Iraqi MiG-21F13 No. 534 (007 in Israel), Israel also captured several other fighters of this type. For example, six Algerian MiG-21F13 flying to Egypt landed by mistake at an airfield which was already in the hands of Israel. Israel handed four of them over to the United States. There is also a never officially confirmed theory that the Israeli Air Force maintained a group called the "Soviet Squadron", equipped with Soviet fighters (3 former Syrian MiG-17, the former Egyptian Su-7B, and aforementioned ex-Iraqi MiG-21F13). The squadron was used only for training Israeli pilots to fight against MiGs and was not used in combat, although the MiG-21F13 No. 007 was the only fighter jet in a state of readiness to protect the airspace of Israel during the war of 5 June 1967 (all other operational aircraft were sent to bomb the Arab airfields)[38]. In the 90s, Israel was using several other MiG-21MF, MiG-21UM and MiG-21bis aircraft, which served as prototypes for modernization by IAI[39].

On 11 October 1989 Syrian pilot Maj. Abdel Bassem landed his MiG-23ML No. 2786 at the Israeli civilian airport of Megido. It had no missiles, but its cannon might have been loaded. It had crossed the Syrian border by flying at a height of a few meters at a speed of about 1,800 km/h[40]. It was a deliberate hijacking in order to leave Syria for religious reasons. The first test flight in Israel was performed on 29 January 1990. It was then presented in the air to the public during Israeli Aviation Day. After tests had been completed it was handed over to the museum in Hatzerim[41]. Israeli forces were interested especially in combat equipment of the MiG-23, the more so that in addition to the radar, it had also a system for tracking airborne targets using infrared.

The electronic equipment of this aircraft was, however, more modest than expected, although the presentation of the radar image displayed on the glass of the sight (and not on a separate screen inside the instrument panel) was very interesting. Interestingly, the aircraft next to the Israeli markings bore also a set of Syrian insignia.

There is also information that in 1990 a Syrian pilot escaped in his MiG-29 fighter to Israel, where the plane was supposedly tested in 1991[42]. This has not been officially confirmed. Later, in 1997 Israel tried two or three MiG-29s on loan from

---

[37] S. Poms, *The aircraft that fell in the hands of the IAF throughout the years have answered some questions regarding the enemies' capabilities*, 2015, http://www.iaf.org.il/4418-44740-en/IAF.aspx.

[38] Y. Efrati, *Colors & markings…*, p. 34.

[39] Y. Gordon, K. Dexter, D. Komissarov, *Mikoyan MiG-29…*, p. 603–604.

[40] http://fly.historicwings.com/2015/04/defection-to-israel/

[41] J. Gruszczyński, E. F. Rybak, C. Piotrowski, M. Wasielewski, *MiG-23 Wersje myśliwskie*, ed. Magnum-X, Warsaw, 1999, p. 69.

[42] Y. Gordon, *Mikoyan MiG-29…*, p. 485, 500.

Poland[43]. These aircraft came from the Polish 1st Fighter Regiment "Warszawa" from Mińsk Mazowiecki. At the turn of April and May 1997 they were lent to the research centre of Israeli Air Force – 601 Squadron/253 Tajaset (Wing) in the Negev desert[44]. For about two weeks they were tested by Israeli pilots. Probably they operated from Ramon airbase.

The Israelis tried to learn all the features of the MiG-29, as it was in the arsenals of Iraq and Syria and a number of other potentially dangerous states. Experienced Israeli pilots had no problems in mastering the MiG-29. During their stay in Israel the Polish MiGs had their national checkerboard markings and the emblem of the 1st PLM overpainted (the original numbers were left). The insignia of the Israeli research centre were painted temporarily on the vertical fins[45]. Initially, the visit of Polish MiG-29s to Israel was kept secret. After a few years, however, information about the event appeared in the specialist press.

1.5. Joint exercises with Polish and Israeli F-16s in March 2012

The MiG-29s of the 1st PLM were not the last Polish fighters on Israeli soil. For some time, Israel has been trying to maintain a relatively extensive cooperation with the air forces of NATO countries, including Poland. Between 7 and 16 March 2012 Polish F-16C participated in the "Desert Hawk" exercises together with Israeli F-15s and F-16Is. They operated from Ovda airbase in the Negev desert. Information about the planned arrival of the Poles was first reported by the "Israel Hayom" newspaper, citing government sources. The Altair Agency described the exercises[46]: There were the simulated dogfights against Israeli F-15s and F-16Is from "The Flying Dragon" squadron. In Israel, missions at low altitude with the use of weapons are possible while they are difficult to implement not only in Poland but throughout Europe. For the Israeli pilots it was important, in turn, to train with NATO pilots.

During the exercises the commanding officer of the Polish Air Force Gen. Lech Majewski was in Israel. He met with the commanding officer of the IAF Maj. Gen. Amir Eshel. Deputy commander of "The Flying Dragon", Maj. Roy said that the exercise was an opportunity to familiarize themselves with the procedures applicable in NATO, and in particular with activities outside their own country, including codes

---

[43]   The quantity of two MiG-29s on loan from Poland is given by Y. Gordon, *Mikoyan MiG-29...*, p. 483, while M. Bogdański in an article *MiG-29 w Polsce* („Aeroplan" No. 5–6 / 2006, Special edition – Monograph on the MiG-29) on p. 13 says that three Polish MiG-29s were sent, numbered 105, 114 and 115. See also: N. Czajkowski, D. Sałata, K. Sałara, A. Wrona, *Polskie MiGi w Izraelu*, w: "Skrzydlata Polska", IssueNo. 05/2012 and N. Ofir, U. Ezion, N. Avrutov, *The „Sting' has landed*, IAF Magazine, http://www.iaf.org.il/5642-35655-en/IAF.aspx

[44]   601 Squadron/Flight Test Center, Negev Squadron, also known as Manat (Hebr. Merkaz Nisu'ey Tisa).

[45]   T. Królikiewicz, R. Gretzyngier, *Polski samolot i barwa 1943–2016, ed.* Bellona, Warsaw, 2016, p. 144.

[46]   *Polskie F-16 w Izraelu*, Altair 17.04.2015,h ttp://www.altair.com.pl/news/view?news_id=7512.

and doctrines. "We were able to verify the international coordination patterns" he said. During the exercises the simulators for surface-to-air missiles and launching vehicles were used. Aircraft also were launching flares. Exercises were held in conditions simulating electronic warfare. Earlier, the Israelis had practiced with the aircraft from Greece, Romania, Italy and the USA. To some extent, they are a substitute for Turkish aircraft, which for years were the main partners for the Israelis, until a political conflict occurred. In parallel with the exercises with Polish F-16, the Israeli air force conducted combat operations over the Gaza Strip.

In an earlier article, the Altair Aviation Agency said: *For the first time the possible joint exercises was announced in late February 2011. Defence Ministers of Poland and Israel signed the declaration on defense cooperation. It was to include, among others, defense industry, training and support for the F-16 aircraft, as well as cooperation in training of special forces. For 2011, eight joint projects in this latter field were planned.* Also joint exercises of the F-16 squadrons were announced.

Due to good weather conditions, the extensive combat experience of Israeli Air Force and the ability to implement in the Negev desert exercises it was impossible to carry out over densely inhabited areas in Europe, the Ovda base is of interest to air forces of many countries. 115 Squadron (also known as the "Flying Dragons") is stationed there on a daily basis, equipped with F-16 fighter jets and Apache attack helicopters, which play the role of aggressors. (…)

Israeli aircraft were in Poland in 2003 during the Radom Air Show. Three F-15 fighter jets flew over the site of the former Nazi concentration camp Auschwitz-Birkenau. One of their pilots was the present commander of the air forces of Israel Maj. Gen. Amir Eshel.

Israel is the only country representing the European mentality in the Middle East. It is no wonder that the state is trying to maintain broad cooperation with Europe and America. The Israeli Air Force will undoubtedly pursue cooperation with NATO air forces, so it can not be ruled out that the planes marked with the Polish checkerboard and Israeli Star of David will meet yet again during allied exercises.

1.6. Polish aircraft in the Israeli-Arab wars

Worth mentioning is the role of the former communist Polish People's Republic as a supplier of military aircraft to the Middle East. During the War of Independence of Israel in 1948 the newly formed Israeli army was supported largely by the Soviet Union and its satellites (hence the supplies of Avia S-199 and Spitfire fighters from Czechoslovakia in the late 40's). Stalin in fact hoped that Israel would become a socialist country, which under Soviet domination will become a wedge between the British and French colonies (protectorates) in the Middle East.

However, by the 50's the political orientation of Israel began to move more and more towards Western countries. It initially concerned mainly France and then in the 70's very wide-ranging cooperation with the US was established as well as Western democracies in general.

Opponents of Israel, especially Egypt and Syria, shifted their attention from the Western countries on the USSR. For example, if in the early 1950's the equipment of Arab states' air forces consisted mainly of British aircraft, shortly afterwards aircraft imported from the Soviet Union and its satellites began to dominate. The contemporary situation in the aviation Egypt is being described by A. Zbiegniewski1[47]: *In June 1967 the Egyptian aviation already had a strongly "sovietized" structure. Traces of the not so old links with the Royal Air Force had been sent into oblivion. From the wide shoulder straps through harmonizing ranks with other types of armed forces[48] up to the regimental structure – everything stressed the ever stronger entrance into the orbit of influence of the Great Red Brother. The best units of EAF (Egyptian Air Force) gathered at the three main airbases in the Suez Canal Zone: Alin Sueir, Fayid and Kabrit. The latter, numbered 228, hosted in their hangars the machines of 12th Air Regiment, composed of three fighter squadrons (18th, 25th and 31st). Contrary to common belief, this was the only Egyptian regiment using MiG-17s. More interestingly, these were mostly Polish Lim-5s. The outbreak of war found the EAF in anticipation of a massive rearmament to the MiG-21s and Su-7s.*

The majority of Lims of 12th Regiment reclassified from interceptors to ground attack aircraft, and were equipped with underwing mountings for unguided missiles.

The same author gives an example of air combat involving a Lim-5P fighter (Polish manufactured MiG-17PF[49]) equipped with an RP-5 Izumrud radar, which left the WSK Mielec's production line in December 1960. It was one of the last produced Lim-5s (in Poland 129 such aircraft were built)[50].

Unfortunately, details on the likely export of Lim-5s (MiG-17s) from Poland to Egypt are still not known. Egypt probably bought those planes second hand (eg. from the Polish armed forces or another country[51]) and not directly from the manufacturer.

Teofil Lenartowicz, a former engineer of WSK Mielec, who was dealing among others with servicing exported Lims mentions that Mielec did not sell any Lim to

---

[47] A. Zbiegniewski, *MiG-i z bazy 228,* in: "Aero" Issue No. 6–7/2007, p. 42.

[48] Earlier the armed forces of Egypt there was in a pattern modelled on the British, where the Army, Royal Air Force and Royal Navy had separate systems of ranks and unit names.

[49] T. Cooper, *How Fighter Pilots Made Modern Syria,* Jan 2017, https://warisboring.com/how-fighter-pilots-made-modern-syria-804f0e1d1283#.pxegj5mez

[50] A. Zbiegniewski, *MiG-i z bazy...,* p. 42–49.

[51] The WSK Mielec plant exported Lim-5/Lim-6 aircraft to the German Democratic Republic, Indonesia and Bulgaria. Egyptian and Syrian MiG-17s were probably repaired at the Military Aviation Factory in Bydgoszcz. See M. Fiszer, J. Gruszczyński, *Historia i współczesność Wojskowych Zakładów Lotniczych nr 2 S.A.,* in: "Lotnictwo LAI" Issue No. 5/2016.

the Middle East. Of the possible export of Lims by the Polish armed forces he has not heard either, and sees this as unlikely.

Lenartowicz does not completely rule out the possibility of obtaining second-hand machines by the Arab states[52]. It cannot be ruled out that Egypt and Syria also purchased in some way Polish MiG-15 variants, i.e.WSK Lim-1/Lim-2s.

Other Polish manufactured aviation equipment were also exported to Egypt and Syria, including SZD-9 Bocian gliders (probably 36 aircraft to Egypt and an un-known number to Syria) which were used for the initial training of military pilots. In the case of aircraft there were An-2s and PZL-104 Wilgas. C. Stafrace says that Egypt bought 24 observation and liaison PZL-104 aircraft in 1975[53]. Whereas R. Kaczkowski[54] gives a figure of only ten Wilgas sold to Egypt. Their buyer was the air force, but temporarily (for transit?) they were given Egyptian civilian registration numbers starting with the letters "SU".

Table 1. The PZL-104 "Wilga 35A" exported to Egypt.

	Buyer: Egyptian Air Force
1)	61141 („251" ex SU-AVB)
2)	61142 („252" ex SU-AVC)
3)	61143 („253" ex SU-AVD)
4)	61144 („254" ex SU-AVE)
5)	61145 („255" ex SU-AVF)
6)	61146 („256" ex SU-AVG)
7)	61147 („257" ex SU-AVH)
8)	61148 („258" ex SU-AVI)
9)	62149 („259" ex SU-AVJ)
10)	62150 („260" ex SU-AVK)

The first 5 digits represent the serial number. In gives the military tactical numbers – painted on the fuselage in Arabic numerals and the temporary civilian registrations.

Source: R. Kaczkowski, "Samolot PZL-104 Wilga", ed. WKŁ, Warsaw, 1983, p. 152

It is however certain that Syria acquired MiG-21F13s which had been previ-ously used in Poland. After the huge losses incurred in the Six Day War, air forces of Syria and Egypt sought ways to obtain new combat aircraft[55]. In addition to

---

[52] Information obtained during a personal interview with Mr. Lenartowicz who serviced, among others, Lim-5Ps in Indonesia. He is the author of the memoir: T. Lenartowicz, *100 lat przygody Mielca z lotnictwem*, Mielec, 2015 and runs a website "My life and the plane – what a mechanic knows of aviation" (http://cowiemechanikolotnictwie.blogspot.com/).

[53] C. Stafrace, *Arab Air Forces*, ed. Squadron-Signal, USA 1994, p. 32.

[54] R. Kaczkowski, *Samolot PZL-104 Wilga*, ed. WKŁ, Warsaw, 1983, p. 152

[55] As early as 1967 a batch of 25 aircraft of the 67 contracted MiG-21PFMs was not delivered on time, because they were sent to the Middle East. See: S. Bartosik, M. Łaz, R. Senkowski, *MiG-21F-13 w służbie*

the USSR, a certain amount of military equipment exported there originated from other Eastern Bloc countries, including the Polish People's Republic. Egypt also received financial support from the Persian Gulf countries. Initially, interest in Polish MiG-21s was expressed by Egypt. Gen. Hassan from the Egyptian army, technical adviser to the Minister of Defense, informed a representative of Polish Cenzin arms trade organization affiliated to the Ministry of Foreign Trade, that his country was interested in buying Polish MiG-21s, T-55 tanks and SKOT armoured personnel carriers. In response, Chief of Import and Export Bureau of the General Staff Col. Henryk Boratyński proposed to sell Egypt 19 MiG-21F-13 fighters, which as it was then described: *we feel a serious lack of spare parts and we have great difficulty in securing their operations and maintenance.* The deal eventually fell through, and the aircraft remained with 2th Fighter Regiment[56].

According to various sources, Egypt had at the time a fleet of 150 to 260 MiG-21s (including non-operational aircraft). Syria had 10 squadrons of over 100 MiG-21s, 60–70% operational. The MiG-21F13s and MiG-21PFs prevailed, but among them were more modern MiG-21MFs. To this must also be added MiG-21 aircraft of the Iraqi forces.

In connection with the outbreak of the Yom Kippur War from 6th to 9th October 1973 military equipment from the Soviet Union, Czechoslovakia, Hungary, East Germany and Poland was supplied, including Polish MiG-21F13s.

Polish MiG-21F13s of the 2. PLM from Goleniów performed their last combat patrol on 13 October 1973. Out of 17 of them, the aviation engineering service selected 12 suitable for sale. The remaining five were stored. These first 12 MiGs flew to Powidz, where after having been dismantled, were loaded onto Soviet An-12 transport aircraft. The question of selection of Polish personnel is described an article in "Lotnictwo", Issue No. 12/2008[57]: *At the same time the personnel to travel abroad was selected. Composition of the delegated staff was agreed with the relevant departments of the Air Force Command. In total, a group numbering 34 people was organized on 16 October, the team was led by a group composed of Lieutenant Colonel MSc Aleksander Werle – comander, Lt. Col. Józef Twaróg – deputy for political affairs, Lt. Col. Stanisław Bryl – deputy for personal and organizational affairs, Lt. Col. Eng. Bernard Życzkowski – deputy for technical affairs, Lt. Col. Ryszard Góra – the doctor. Flying personel consisted of three pilots from the 2nd PLM: Maj. Zbigniew Biedrzycki, Cpt. Czesław Stawski, Cpt. Szymon Krupa. Technical staff, originating from units of the 4th Fighter Division (2nd PLM from Goleniów and 45th Field Workshop from Malbork), represented all the technical aviation specialties. In total, a group of 23 men*

---

polsko-syryjskiej, in: "Lotnictwo" Issue No. 12/2008, p. 57. See also: Y. Gordon, K. Dexter, D. Komissarov, *Mikoyan MiG-21...*, p. 670–673.

[56]   S. Bartosik, M. Łaz, R. Senkowski, *MiG-21F-13...*, p. 57.

[57]   *Ibidem*, p. 58

consisting of 7 officers, 4 warrant officers and 12 NCO's. There were also representa-
tives of counterintelligence – two officers and a non-commissioned officer from the
2nd Department, General Staff.

The whole project was top secret. Pilots were only informed about a "task to perform
in the Middle East."

The technical staff had even less knowledge. In Goleniów because of the need to
prepare the equipment, it was clear, at least, what was the subject of the task. Staff of
45th Field Workshop from Malbork did not even know what tasks they would perform
nor of course where. It was not allowed to take any personal belongings, even clothes
and a toothbrush. Each group received money to buy everything they needed on the
spot. The cargo was not well known to all, because the aircraft had been dismantled
in Powidz by another team which was to stay in Poland.

The first six An-12s took off from Powidz on 18 October. These aircraft sported
civilian Aeroflot colour scheme, though they came from a military transport regiment stationed in Lithuania. They transported a group of staff with the exception
of the pilots, four disassembled MiG-21F13s and ancillary equipment. Two days
later another five AN-12s set off from Powidz. They transported flying personnel
and a further 4 MiG-21F13s with a set of spare parts. The last four An-12 with four
MiGs took off from Powidz on 21 October. The Soviet Antonov transport aircraft
flew over Wrocław and Prague, and then landed at Soviet airbase in Budapest. For
this journey the Soviet crews were equipped with small arms, which raised concern
among the Poles transported by them. Further route was over Sarajevo, Dubrovnik,
Adriatic Sea and Ionian Sea, all the way to Syria. When passing Crete and Cyprus the
Antonovs were approached by American F-4 Phantoms which accompanied them
for several minutes. The flight took place at an altitude of 7000 m and at a distance
of about 200 km from the coast of Syria, it was lowered to the height of 300–500
m. From that moment on blackout and radio silence procedures were maintained.
The Syrian shoreline was crossed between Latakia and Homs.

The entire flight from Budapest took about 6–6.5 hours and ended up by landing
at Aleppo, located about 70 km from the border with Turkey and about 150 km
from the Mediterranean Sea. Only then did the Poles learn that they had come
to Syria[58].

The Poles were not the only foreigners there. There were also two groups of
Soviets (military and civilian) of about 70 men assembling MiG-21MFs, a group
from the GDR composed of 60 technical personnel and 12 pilots assembling 12
MiG-21Ms, a group of Hungarians assembling 15 MiG-21F13s and a civilian
Czechoslovak group of about 50 men assembling 12 MiG-21F13s (license built in
Czechoslovakia as the Aero S-106).

---

[58] S. Bartosik, M. Łaz, R. Senkowski, *MiG-21F-13…, p. 58.*

There was the risk of Israeli air strike, so there was a blackout at night (the day before the arrival of the Poles the base was attacked by Israeli F-4 Phantoms, which destroyed one of the Soviet An-12s). Runway lights were switched on only at the time of landing, after the fourth turn have been made by a landing aircraft.

The local conditions were as follows[59]: *The base commander was General. Brig. Madjeb Hamchu who the next morning, ie. on 19 October contacted the Polish group with Col. Adnan responsible for organizing accommodation and jobs at the base. To work began at 11.00 hours, but from the next day they worked from dawn to dusk, that is, from 04.30 to 18.00 hours. It would probably have been longer, if not for the total blackout at night. The conditions were onerous, as in the field, the aircraft were assembled under the open sky. Frequent alarms forced them to push in and pull out the planes from the hangar. From 20 October, with the help of the head of the Soviet group Col. Afanasyev Antonovich Syedych, assembly work proceeded smoothly. In turn, the support of the local authorities was limited initially to assign ten soldiers, quite unqualified and generally reluctant to work. Moreover, during the period of Ramadan from 08.00 to 16.00 hours they were sleeping through the whole day near the hangars with no reaction from their superiors. Only two non-commissioned officers were willing to assist who had been trained in servicing MiG-17s. As time passed, the Syrians provided a mechanical workshop. On 24 October the first test flight of three aircraft took place. Successively over the coming days, the remainder were taken into the air. The test flights were treated as combat missions, as they were held in conditions full of danger for the base and surrounding area. Therefore, the aircraft were armed with R-3S guided missiles and loaded cannons. The pilots were advised to commence fighting if encountering Israeli aircraft. Therefore, for each flight, Maj. Biedrzycki, Cpt. Krupa and Capt. Stawski were preparing like for a regular combat mission.*

The role of advisor was played by a Soviet pilot Col. Anatol. It is also worth noting that radio communication in the air were carried out in the Syriac language by using commands that pilots had to learn by heart. After test flights the planes were inspected, refuelled and after the extra fuel tank had been fitted, on the same day they were transferred to the paint shop. There, within 12 hours they were given camouflage schemes and Syrian markings, and afterwards deployed to frontline airfields. Aircraft were piloted by Soviets dressed in Syrian uniforms.

On 4 November a Polish military An-12at Aleppo landed, commanded by Maj. Henryk Bajer from the 13th Air Transport Regiment, who brought new wings for one of the MiG-21F13, which had been damaged during assembly.

On 21 October the Syrians submitted a proposal to the Polish pilots in Syria to take part in the fighting at the front. However, this was met with a refusal by the Polish Ministry of Defence. Approval from their Ministry of Defence was received

---

[59]   *Ibidem*, p. 59

for the pilots from the German Democratic Republic. It is not known whether they saw action, though.

The return of Polish personnel took place in two groups. The first group of 23 men reached Powidz on 1 November aboard two An-12s in Aeroflot livery. During the flight, between Cyprus and Crete they met American F-4 Phantoms in the air and at sea a flotilla of 16 ships sailing eastward was noticed. The second group of Poles returned on 9 November on a Polish An-12 of the 13th PLT (Aviation Transport Regiment), which flew over Turkey and the Black Sea, and eventually landed at Powidz.

The ex-Polish MiG-21F13s did not take part in the Yom Kippur war, but undoubtedly participated in later battles, when most likely the Israeli fighter planes shot down some of them. The contemporary service of MiG-21s in Syria according to the authors of the aforementioned article: *In 1973–1974 the MiG-21F-13s were assigned to several Syrian squadrons: 7th at Latakia, 8th and 10th at Damascus, 11th and 67th at Dumayr and 68th at Marij Sultan. It is known that Eastern European production aircraft formed at least the 67th Squadron at Dumayr. Pilots from Syria and Pakistan served with this unit. On 19 April 1974 fighting broke out between Israeli Mirage IIICJs and MiG-21F-13s of the 67th Squadron. As a result, one MiG-21F-13 fell victim to a Shafrir Mk 2 guided missile, while the other was hit by a burst from a Mirages cannon. Perhaps these were Polish machines. Ten days later, there was another duel in which Israeli F-4Es armed with AIM-7F and AIM-9D missiles sent to the ground next four Syrian MiG-21s of unspecified versions. (…)*

After the end of the Yom Kippur War 80 aircraft of older versions remained in reserve, mainly MiG-21F-13s, complementing the losses incurred in 1973. This is how the aircraft from Eastern Europe, including ex-Polish ones, ended their service record with the Syrian air force (if they had not previously fallen victim to the fighters with Stars of David).

It is worth mentioning about the crash of the Polish Antonov An-12 transport aircraft in Beirut (Lebanon) on 13 May 1977. This aircraft belonged to the Polish armed forces, but had civilian registration SP-LZA[60] and formally was a flight number 6883, as a Polish "LOT" airlines plane. The plane took off from Warsaw and flew to Beirut with a stopover in Varna. The commander of the aircraft was Maj. Henryk Bajer[61] who had spent 6,000 hours in the air.

---

[60] „Aviation Safety" website reports that it had a serial number 6344307 See: http://aviation-safety. net/database/record.php?id=19770513-0. It was probably the An-12, which in its military livery sported number 50. Photos of Polish An-12 SP-LZA or 50 can be found in: J. R. Konieczny, "Samolot transportowy An-12" – "Typy Broni i Uzbrojenia" series No. 23, ed. MON, Warsaw, 1973. See also: M. Mikulski, A. Glass, *Polski transport lotniczy 1918–1978*, ed. WKŁ, Warsaw, 1980 and A. Jońca, *Barwa w lotnictwie polskim*, Part 5: *Samoloty linii lotniczych 1957–1981*, ed. WKŁ, Warsaw, 1986, p. 14–15.

[61] As stated previously, on 4 November 1973 Maj. H. Bajer commanded a military An-12 of 13th PLT which landed at the Syrian city of Aleppo, where he brought wings for one of the MiG-21F13s, which had been damaged during assembly.

The plane approached runway No. 21 at Beirut, and had come down to 1,500 feet (about 460 metres). At about 08.50 the plane crashed 8 km from the runway threshold, near the village of Aramoun, hitting a nearby mountain. As a result of the crash nine people were killed (all those who were on board).

Among the causes of this tragedy are given incorrect reading of bearings NDB beacon by the crew, and errors on the part of the Lebanese approach control at the airport in Beirut. The pilots of the plane, however, were very experienced and it is unlikely they made such a mistake. Officially, the aircraft brought strawberries from Lebanon while performing a commercial flight (during the communist times planes owned by the military were allowed to make commercial flights, which today is completely impossible). Some time later, there were suspicions that perhaps this plane was carrying weapons. According to reports, published by "Newsweek"[62], the An-12 in addition to 12 tons of beef, it could have carried medicines and guns for sale to the Lebanese (this theory has never been proven). A factor contributing to the crash could also be overworking the crew, as they were flying very much. There was also a theory that the plane could have been shot down by guerillas to prevent the supply of weapons to Lebanon. This has never been proven either.

Probably they are not the only threads in the history of Polish aviation in Israel, Syria and Egypt. However, despite the passage of decades, there are still many details that are shrouded in mystery. Perhaps with time new facts will see the light.

---

[62] P. Semczuk, *1977 Zapomniany lot 6883*, "Newsweek", 01.12.2009, http://historia.newsweek. pl/1977-zapomniany-lot-6883,49643,1,1.html and „13 maja 1977 – Zapomniany lot 6883 do Bejrutu", "Krakowski Oddział Stowarzyszenia Seniorów Lotnictwa Wojskowego RP", http://www.kosslwrp.republika.pl/www/html/historia.htm.

The beginnings of aviation in the British Mandate of Palestine

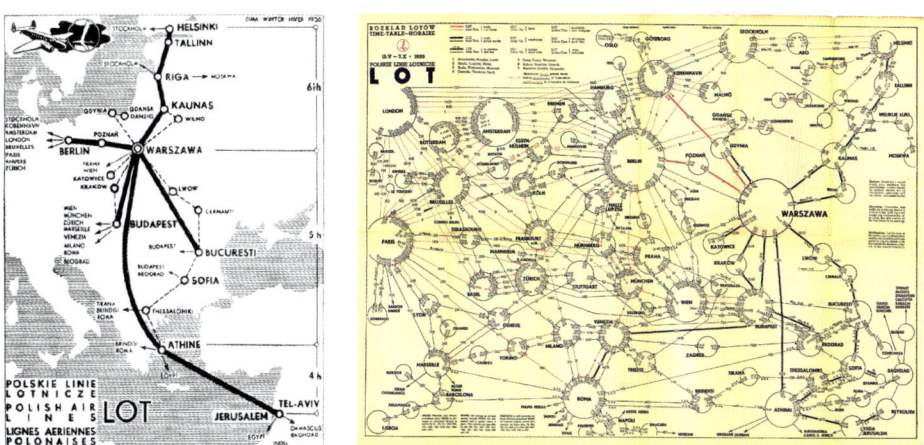

Maps of the LOT Polish Airlines destinations in the late 30's, note the connections
the Middle East

The Douglas DC-2 aircraft, SP-ASK of the LOT Polish Airlines at the airport of Lydda in
Palestine, the late 30's

The Douglas DC-2 SP-ASL of the LOT Polish Airlines at the airport of Lydda in Palestine, late 30's

The first group of Haganah pilots in front of Polish production RWD-8 training aircraft near the Afikim (pilots: Yitzhak Ben Yaakov, Imanuel Zuckerman-Tzur, engineer Pohorille, Dov Hoz and others)

Polish production aircraft RWD-8 VQ-PAK and RWD-13 (still with the Polish registration SP-BFM) near Kibbutz Afikim in 1938. The RWD-13 was the first aircraft in the history of Israel, which performed a combat mission

Training of Haganah airmen on the RWD 8 VQ-PAB, probably around the Kibbutz Revivim.

The Palestinian (Jewish) RWD-13 and RWD-15 (VQ-PAE)

An interesting image of the Egyptian Dragon Rapide SU-ABQ of the Misr airlines, the British Armstrong Whitworth Atalanta G-ABTJ of the Imperial Airways and three-engined Fokker F.XVIII with Palestinian registration VQ-PAF. This aircraft first served with Dutch KLM, then with Czechoslovakian CSA, and in December 1938 it was sold to Commercial Aviation Corporation of Palestine. VQ-PAF crashed near the airport of Lydda on 13 January 1939 r. Its damaged wreckage was later taken over by the Israeli aviation, but never restored and it was eventually scrapped after 1948

British Handley Page HP.42 G-AAGX of the Imperial Airways at the airport of Lydda, the early 30's

Egyptian De Havilland Dragon Rapide SU-ABS of the Misr airlines refuelling next to the Short S.16 Scion (VQ-PAA or VQ-PAB) of the Palestine Airways Ltd from Jerusalem, Lydda Airport, the early 30's

Air combat in 1948

Israeli Piper Cub flying over own troops 1948

The shot down Egyptian Spitfire Mk.IX in the vicinity of Tel Aviv, 1948

Distribution of oil in the engines by turning the propellers before the takeoff of the Israeli B-17

The Israeli pilots (including Lou Lenart) at the Avia S-199 fighter

Advertisment of "Above and Beyond. The Untold True Story" movie on the first combat actions by Israeli Air Force. Note the Messershmitt Bf-109E masuerading as the S-199

The Avia S-199, in fact the Messershmitt Bf-109G with Junkers Jumo 211F, capacity of 1,322 hp

The Israeli troops at the wreckage of an Egyptian Spitfire

The first Israeli airmen in front of the C-46 Commando, Panamanian registration RX-134

Douglas C-54B 4X-ACA (the ex-US N58021) at the base in Ekron in 1948. It was the first aircraft in the civil register of independent Israel. It crashed on 2 January 1949 having tried to land at Tel Aviv

Syrian Gloster Meteor.

Syrian Fiat G.55 fighter, the late 40's

Wreckage of the Syrian Spitfire F.22.

Syrian Percival P.44 Proctor, most likely belonging to the Governmental Squadron.

The Israeli P-51D Mustang downed during the Suez Crisis, 1956

Israeli Spitfire Mk.IX at the museum in Hatzerim

1948–1958   1961–1963   1963–1972   from 1972

Syrian national recognition markings. 1948-1956 (now in use by the Syrian rebels), 1961–1963, 1963–1972, 1972 to date (in many case even though new regulations had been binding, the previous markings would still be used)

Painted by Bill Dady

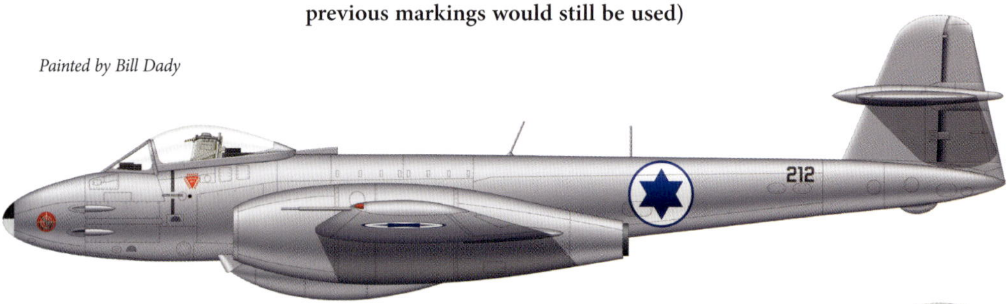

Gloster Meteor F.8 – Israeli Defence Force 1954

Gloster Meteor FR.9 – Israeli Defence Force 1954

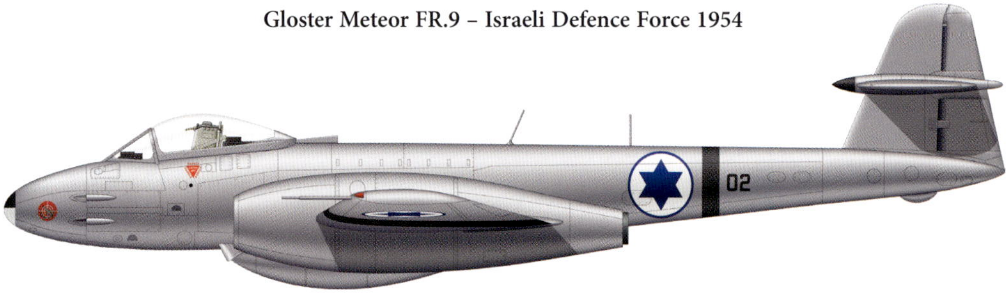

Gloster Meteor F.8 – Israeli Defence Force 1956

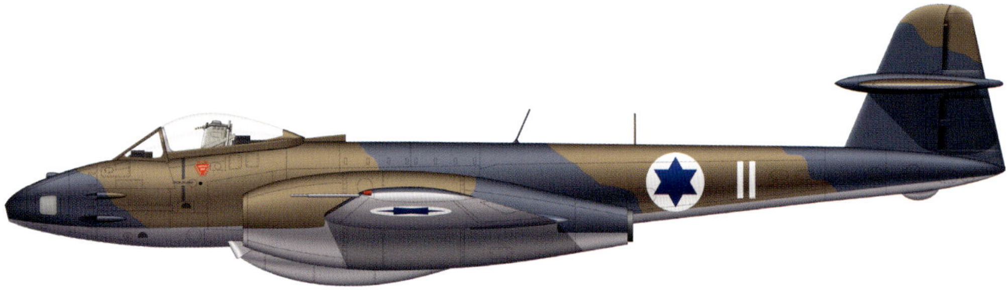

Gloster Meteor FR.9 – Israeli Defence Force 1957

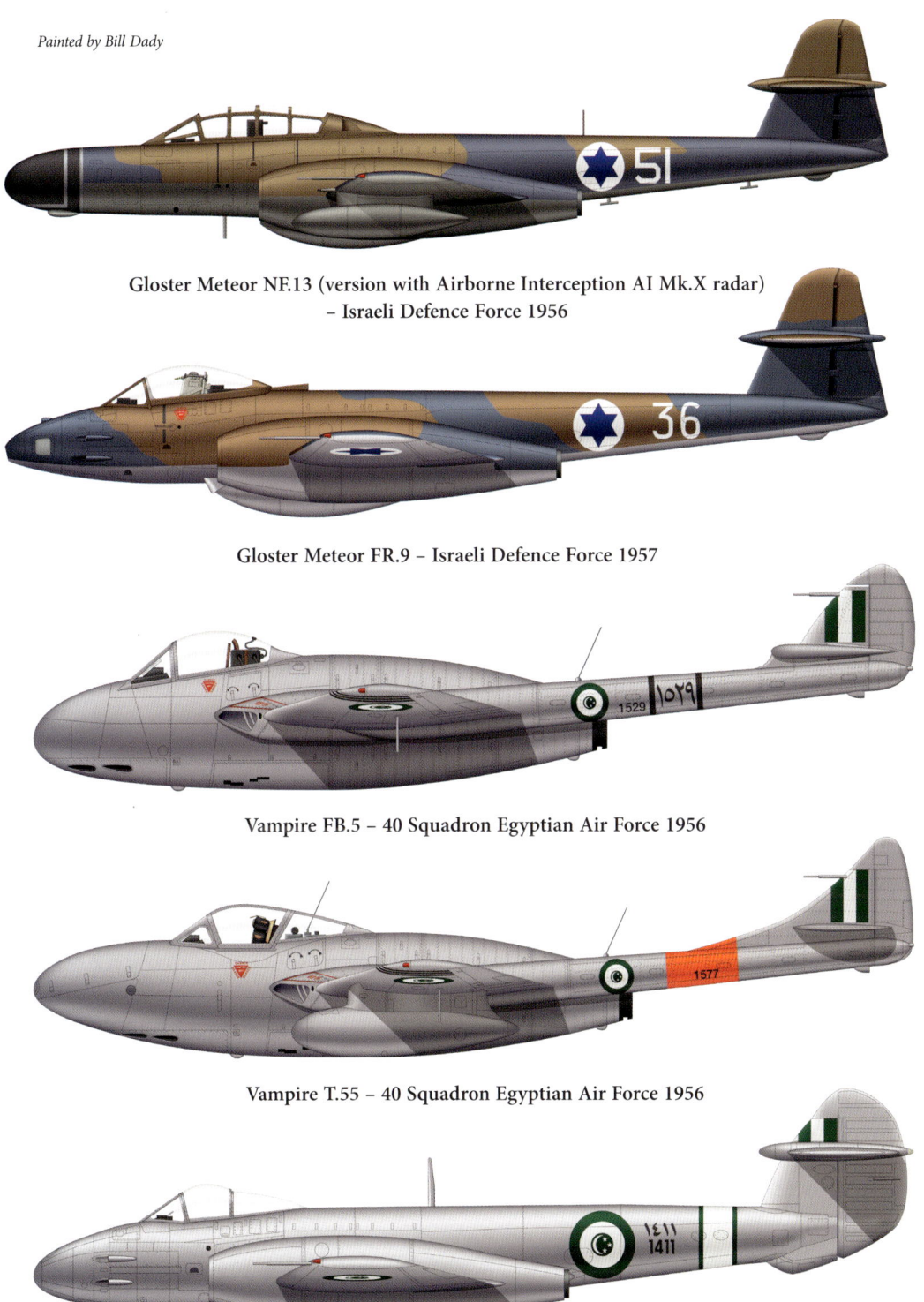

Painted by Bill Dady

Gloster Meteor NF.13 (version with Airborne Interception AI Mk.X radar)
– Israeli Defence Force 1956

Gloster Meteor FR.9 – Israeli Defence Force 1957

Vampire FB.5 – 40 Squadron Egyptian Air Force 1956

Vampire T.55 – 40 Squadron Egyptian Air Force 1956

Gloster Meteor F.4 – Egyptian Air Force 1951

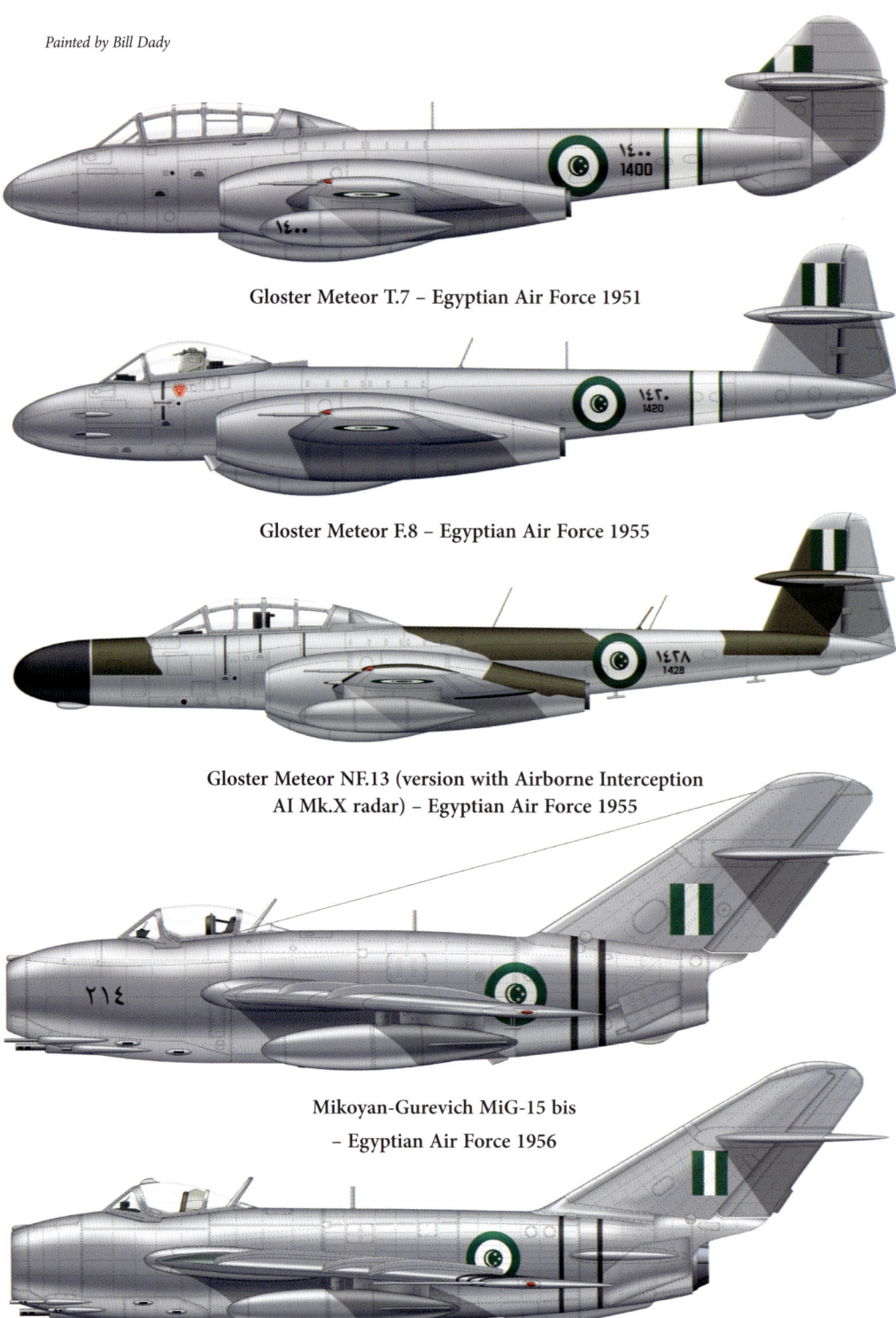

Painted by Bill Dady

Gloster Meteor T.7 – Egyptian Air Force 1951

Gloster Meteor F.8 – Egyptian Air Force 1955

Gloster Meteor NF.13 (version with Airborne Interception
AI Mk.X radar) – Egyptian Air Force 1955

Mikoyan-Gurevich MiG-15 bis
– Egyptian Air Force 1956

Mikoyan-Gurevich MiG-17F – Egyptian Air Force 1966

Painted by Bill Dady

North American P-51D – 101 Squadron Israeli Air Force 1956

North American P-51D – 101 Squadron Israeli Air Force 1956

North American P-51D – 116 Squadron
Israeli Air Force 1956

Chance-Vought Corsair F4U-7 – Flottile F15 French Navy 1956

Westland Wyvern S Mk 4 – 830 Naval Air Squadron 1956

Subsequent development of the Israeli Air Force

The prototype IAI Lavi B-2 at the museum in Hatzerim

Israeli Mirage III BJ used for testing of the ejector seats for the IAI Nesher

Tests of MiG's in Israel

The Israeli test pilot Colonel Danny Shapiro and his MiG-21F13

The same MiG-21F13 at the museum in Hatzerim

The Israeli MiG-21F13 – the „007" – during the air show

Ex-Syrian MiG-17F (or was it its Polish copy LiM-5?) being tested in Israel and the USA

The Israeli MiG-23 and F-16 together. Note the Syrian markings left next to the new Israeli national signs on the MiG. What also brings to attention is the effective camouflage

MiG-21-2000 Lancer or the Israeli-Romanian modification of 1990's

The Israeli MiG-23 and MiG-21F13 at the museum in Hatzerim

Polish MiG-29 „105". Note the national recognition markings
are painted out and the emblem of the Negev Squadron was
added, Israel, April-May, 1997

The Negev Squadron insignia

Joint exercises with Polish and Israeli F-16s in March 2012

Desert Hawk exercise badge

The Polish MiG-29s over Israel, 1997

Polish and Israeli F-16s during Desert Hawk exercise, 2012

The Israeli F-15s over the Nazi German Auschwitz Concentration Camp, 2003

Allied handshake of Polish and Israeli airmen during their visit to Poland in 2003

CHAPTER II

Air Combat of the Air Forces of Israel since 1956

2.1. The Suez Crisis of 1956

The Suez Crisis (Israeli operation "Kadesh"), was a military operation of the United Kingdom, France and Israel against Egypt, which began on 29 October 1956. Aggression had been preceded by Egypt's decision on nationalization of the Suez Canal (26 July 1956). However, the actual cause of the outbreak of war was the desire of Britain and France to maintain control of the Canal. These countries to achieve their goals used Israel, merchant vessels of which had been banned from the Suez Canal. Israel had also its own other good reasons to take part in the war: weakening Egypt and its army so that it would not be able to invade Israel as well as to destroy the militant, which attacked Israeli territory near the border.

The genesis of this conflict can be traced to the history of the Arabs, who in the modern period have not managed to create any very strong power comparable with European or Asian empires[63]. For many centuries they felt dominated by the influence of the West. The decision of Egyptian President G. A. Nasser on nationalization of the Suez Canal had been received in the Arab world as a kind of awakening of the Arabs toward independence from foreign influence and prompted a wave of enthusiasm and support throughout the Middle East. But it was only a formal seal on the earlier facts – already in 1949 after the first Arab-Israeli War had been lost, Egypt closed the Suez Canal to Israeli shipping and blocked the Gulf of Aqaba. In August 1951 British Foreign Minister Anthony Eden gave Egypt full rights to decide on the Suez Canal.

Fuel to the fire had been added by the presence of British forces in Egypt, which despite two agreements (in 1936 and 1946) according to which the British agreed to withdraw by 1949, remained in Egypt into the 50's. On 1 September 1951 UN Security Council issued Resolution No. 95, which called the closure of the Suez Canal

---

[63] Cultural and ideological issues associated with President Nasser and the Suez Canal are described in: Corm G., *Le Proche-Orient eclate 1956-2000*, Gallimard 2010.

"an abuse limiting rights" and called on Egypt to open the Canal for all shipping. In response, in 1951 Egypt cancelled the Egyptian-British agreement of 1936 and forced British troops to leave the Suez Canal zone by 1954. In 1952 Egyptian army officers carried out a coup that ended the rule of the British puppet, King Farouk I, and introduced an aggressive anti-Israel stance. The new Egyptian government also established broad cooperation with the Soviet Union and its allies. By October 1956 from Eastern Bloc countries (mainly the USSR) 230 tanks, 300 armored personnel carriers, 500 guns and mortars, 170 combat aircraft and several ships[64] were delivered to Egypt. In addition Egypt received military equipment purchased by Syria in Italy and Czechoslovakia. So far, the main supplier of arms to Egypt had been the United Kingdom, which after the change of government limited its assistance drastically. For example, British instructors of Egyptian pilots were ordered to train them only on basic principles of fight in air[65]. Egypt was looking for other supply routes – for example, in September 1955 it purchased in Italy a batch of FIAT Vampire FB.52 fighters (license-built British De Havilland Vampire). On 27 September an agreement was signed with Czechoslovakia for supply of 86 MiG-15/MiG-15UTI fighters, 39 Il-28 bombers, 14 Il-20 transports, 20 Avia C-11 (Yak-11) trainers and 200 T-34 tanks. Shortly afterwards, more than 100 MiG-15 were provided and a number of more modern MiG-17. Czechoslovak and Soviet instructors arrived as well[66].

The MiG-15s and MiG-17s in Egypt represented a new level of quality in the Middle East. So far, the United Kingdom had sought to control the local balance of armaments and was providing both parties mainly older-generation equipment. In 1956 the Arabs received some of the most advanced fighter jets in the world, far exceeding the performance of Israeli fighters. The response was not long in coming. Egypt supported the Algerian insurgents against France, so the latter sold Israel its newest fighters – Dassault Ouragan and Mystère II. Although they were inferior to MiG-15s the Israelis made up for these shortcomings by better training of pilots.

In 1955 Egypt managed to pick up a batch of six British NF.13 Meteor fighters, with which a night fighter squadron was formed. From then on mainly Soviet equipment was used. In October 1955 the first MiG-15s entered service with 1st and 30th Squadron based at Almaza in Cairo. At the same time, the 9th Squadron received modern bombers – Ilyushin Il-28. The influx of modern MiGs and Ilyushins was a revolution in aviation for Egypt, which so far had been using far less advanced

---

[64]   H. M. Sachar, *A History of Israel from the Rise of Zionism to Our Time*, ed. Alfred A. Knopf, New York, 1976. Schemes of combat operations in 1956 can be found in: A. Swanson, M. Swanson, *Military Atlas of Air Warfare*, 2014 and A. Balint, I. Szabo, *Atlas współczesnych konfliktów zbrojnych*, ed. Buchmann, Warsaw, 2012, p. 14–15.

[65]   Description of the events during the Suez crisis were based mainly on: T. Cooper, *Suez Crisis in 1956*, ACIG, 2009 http://www.acig.info/CMS/.

[66]   R. Ball says that Naser in 1955 bought 120 MiG-15s, 50 Il-28s and 20 Il-14s. See idem, *The Israeli Air Force...*, p. 42.

machines. This caused a lot of problems to overcome the need for which was the time. However, there was very little time, as the potential enemy – Israel – also adopted new technologies in its armed forces. For example, in May, Israel bought 18 French fighter aircraft Dassault Mystere IVA. In August, another batch of 36 Mystères and 6 Ouragans was delivered. In the UK three Gloster Gladiator NF.13 were acquired.

Egypt was very quickly gaining a military advantage over Israel, which caused an increase in confidence among the Egyptians and on 2 March 1956 President Nasser demanded that Israel restore the borders set in UN Security Council Resolution No. 181 of 1947. At the turn of June and July 1956 the last British troops left Egypt, and on 26 July 1956 President Nasser announced the nationalization of the Suez Canal. 44% of the Suez Canal Company's shares were held by British companies and banks. At the time of the nationalization everything became the property of the treasury of Egypt. Then the Egyptians imposed high fees, which in practice halted shipping on the Canal.

On 22–24 October 1956 the United Kingdom, France and Israel signed the so-called Protocol of Sèvres, which had assumed that Israel would invade the Sinai peninsula, while France and the United Kingdom would act as the formal concili-ators and would enter Egypt officially to separate the warring parties, taking the opportunity to regain control over the Suez Canal.

In June 1956 the last British troops left Egypt. A month later, the United States refused to finance the construction of a dam at Aswan and the Egyptian Government in response took over the managing organization of Canal, the Suez Canal Corpora-tion. This caused a shock in the UK and France, operation "Railcar" was developed according to which 80,000 troops were to be transferred to Egypt tasked to capture Alexandria and Cairo. Later, the plan was limited only to seizing the Suez Canal area and was renamed "Musketeer." The plan called for the bombing of certain facilities in Egypt, and the occupation of a narrow strip of Egyptian territory, allowing regaining control over the Canal. On 1 September France suggested that Israel should be invited to participate in this joint operation. The British were initially opposed to this because they had been afraid of the excessive growth of this young state in the Middle East. Finally, Israel was invited to collaborate on 29 September. It was decided that the op-eration would start with an Israeli attack on Egyptian troops in the Sinai, followed by an Anglo-French mediation ultimatum directed to both sides of the conflict. Forces of both sides were to withdraw to a distance of at least 18 km from Suez. For western countries it was obvious that the Egyptians would not agree to this arrangement, and the continued presence of their forces at the Canal was to be a pretext to launch the invasion. Of course, all this was kept a closely guarded secret. The British had, in fact hopes to maintain good relations with the Arab world. While their relations with Israel were still so tense that even armed intervention against it had not been excluded, if Israel would decide to attack Jordan. This operation was codenamed "Cordage" and planned ferrying DH Venom FB.4 fighters to Amman, Malta and Cyprus in order to raid Israeli airbases[67]. HM Government was ready to carry out both operations ("Musketeer" and "Cordage"), should the need arise. The Royal Navy was intended to use against Israel among other vessels the light cruiser HMS Royalist, because she had very modern radar guided anti-aircraft weapons, capable to defend against Israeli Mysteres. Eventually, the ship went to New Zealand, and no fighting between the British and the Israelis occurred.

After Israel had been admitted to operation "Musketeer" the air force of that country was strengthened. France provided at least 12 more Ouragans and 23 additional Mystere IVAs. In mid-1956 Israel announced it had 176 combat aircraft, including 112 jets. The elite 101st Squadron already had 52 Mystere IV As, but so far only 16 trained pilots. The next ones were trained on extraordinary brief courses. 113th Squadron had 24 Ouragans and the 115th and 117th the older British Meteor fighters. Two other squadrons flew the already archaic P-51D Mustangs. Transport aviation boasted aircraft C-47/DC-3 Dakota aircraft and the newer Nord Noratlas. At that time, the Israeli air force had 131 pilots, including 53 trained on jets. The Israeli high command believed that their air force was able to destroy the Egyptian air force. The British and French were skeptical, recognizing that Israel's air force may not be in a position even to defend their own country. Some Israeli politicians shared this opinion.

The British did not wish larger amounts of French equipment to be stationed in Cyprus, so the French had to switch a few units to Israel. These were 18 Mystere IVAs of EC.1/2 Cigone, EC.2/2 Cote d'Or and EC.3/2 Alsace, which were transferred to Haifa on 23 October. These aircraft received Israeli markings and formed the fictional Israeli 199th Squadron. A day later, in Israel there were also French Republic F-84F Thunderstreak fighters of EC.1/1 Corse, EC.2/1 Morvan and EC.3/1 Argonne, which flew in via Cyprus. These formed the fictional Israeli 200th Squadron. Initially, the French were only to protect Israeli territory against air raids (especially the feared IL-28 bombers), but later they would actively join in the fighting.

All members of the western coalition were seeking the possibility of destruction of the Egyptian air force while still on the ground, before they could take off. It was recognized that the MiG-15 and MiG-17 fighter aircraft outperformed western aircraft. Another concern was also the fact that the Il-28 bombers could reach British bases in Cyprus. This would be a very attractive target for the Egyptians, because the base was jam-packed with aircraft (especially British). Therefore, destruction of the enemy's strike potential as soon as possible was extremely important.

---

[67] T. Cooper, *Suez Crisis...*; M. Templeton, *Ties of Blood and Empire: New Zealand's Involvement in Middle East Defence and the Suez Crisis 1947–1957*, ed. Auckland University Press, Auckland, New Zealand 1994, p. 130–131.

In reality though, the combat capabilities of the Egyptian aviation were limited. In the summer of 1956 it was led by Air Vice Marshall[68] Sodky and was composed of about 6,400 men, divided into two Commands: the Eastern responsible for defending the border with Israel in the Sinai and the Central responsible for the Nile delta and Cairo. The Egyptian air force was in the process of re-armament from equipment of British origin to modern Soviet aircraft. Egypt still had a fleet of 90 British DH Vampire and 30 Gloster Meteor (both of World War II vintage), but 120 new MiG-15s and MiG-17s were being introduced to service. The Egyptians had too few qualified personnel, hence only about 60% of combat aircraft were operational. For example, the 2nd Squadron at El-Arish had 18 operational Vampires and a further 12 unfit to fly. 8th and 9th Squadron at Inchas had 39 Ilyushin Il-28 bombers, but only 24 were in operational condition. 30th Squadron at Devorsoir has just completed training on the MiG-15s, but was not yet fully operational. Two more squadrons were in process of training on the MiG-15s. Overall, Egypt had then 69 MiG-15s in operational condition. The 1st Squadron of Devorsoir was also training on the very modern and extremely dangerous MiG-17s, the squadron had 12 aircraft of this type.

At the end of October 1956 Egypt already had at least 150 fighter jets and 39 Il-28 jet bombers, as well as 440 pilots, of whom 110 had been trained on the jets. Additionally, in northern Egypt a network of at least 60 radar sites was built as well as several air defense centres with help of engineers from the Soviet Union and Czechoslovakia. However, the Egyptians did not manage to complete them before start of hostilities. The combat potential of the air forces of Israel and Egypt were then comparable. Egypt had better aircraft, but their pilots were less well trained in air combat. The Israelis were less disciplined than the Egyptians, but more aggressive. They were among the best-trained pilots in the world. Practice has shown that Mysteres piloted by the Israelis turned out to be a much more effective weapon that the latest MiG-15s and MiG-17s in Egiptian hands. The MiGs turned out to be more maneuverable and had a better rate of climb. Their design was also more bullet-proof than the French fighters which Israel had. The Egyptians had the advantage in ground attack aviation, because every MiG could fire at targets with heavy 23 mm and 37 mm bullets[69], originally designed to destroy heavy bombers. However, both the Israelis and the Egyptians had not yet had much experience in piloting jets.

The Royal Air Force, Fleet Air Arm and the French naval aviation Aeronavale combined had a much larger force than Egypt. However, only the F-84F fighter was

---

[68]   The names of ranks and units followed the British model, but would soon be modified along the Soviet patterns.

[69]   Armament of the MiG-15 and MiG-17: 1 × N-37D gun 37 mm, 2 × NR-23 cannon 23 mm and 500 kg underwing weaponry or 2 fuel tanks of 400 litres.

comparable to MiG-15. The F-84F was even a little faster than the MiG, but was less maneuverable and had inferior firepower[70].

Egypt maintained friendly relations with the anti-British movement in Cyprus. However, this organization failed to warn Egypt of the massive concentration of British forces on the island. British raids from Cyprus and Malta were a huge surprise to the Egyptians. The operation was kept secret until the very last minute even though the preparations had started in August, when the first British Canberra and Valiant bombers were ferried to Malta. Subsequently large numbers of fighter planes were flown to Cyprus until the British bases on the island became overcrowded. In late October, at least 112 combat aircraft were in Akrotiri, 127 at Nicosia and 46 at Tymbou. Among them there were two squadrons of the new Hawker Hunter F. Mk.1s, one night squadron of Gloster Meteor NF.13s, three of the 36 DH Venom fighter-bombers, as well as 60 French F-84Fs and 16 reconnaissance RF-84Fs. Also deployed on Cyprus were Canberra B.Mk.2 bombers and on Malta heavy Vickers Valiants and more Canberras.

In the meantime, substantial naval forces had been collected. In August 1956 the Royal Navy had only one operational aircraft carrier – the newly built HMS Eagle. Two months later, she was joined by several other carriers. HMS Bulwark initially did not have any planes. HMS Centaur was in dry dock and could not be used. HMS Albion was undergoing repairs, but was used as a transport for ferrying troops to Malta. However, Eagle, Bulwark and Albion were already fully operational at the start of operation "Musketeer". In total on decks of these ships there were 163 aircraft, including 117 Hawker Sea Hawk, Sea Venom and Wyvern fighters. In addition, HMS Theseus and HMS Ocean aided the fleet as transports. British for the first time on a large-scale transferred troops onto the coast on helicopters (each of the ships had about 12). This is now a standard procedure in many navies of the world, but in 1956 it was a surprising novelty. In addition to five aircraft carriers, the British fleet consisted of 13 destroyers, six frigates, five submarines and 60 other vessels operating from Malta.

France had an adequate number of ships to conduct the operation, but most of them operated in Indochina at that time. The French task force, which sailed from Cap Bone in Algeria on 27 October consisted of the Arromanches (purchased from the UK in 1948) and LaFayette (on loan from the US since 1951) aircraft carriers. They were equipped with the outdated F4U Corsairs and the equally old TBD Avenger bombers suitable also to hunt for submarines. France sent there her last battleship Richelieu and 20 smaller naval escorts and supply vessels.In the eastern part of the Mediterranean operated also the US 6th Fleet with a significant aircraft carrier component, consisting of the USS Coral Sea (CVB-43), USS Randolph (CVA-

---

[70]   Armament of the F-84F: 6 × Browning M3 cal. 12.7 mm machine guns.

15) and USS Salem (CA-138). The Americans were aware of the concentration of British and French forces, but did not take any action.

Egyptian Navy had much poorer strength. In the early 50's it consisted of two Hunt class destroyers, six frigates and one smaller vessel. All Egyptian ships had been of World War 2 vintage and were purchased in the UK. In 1955 Nasser two modern Soviet destroyers of the Skoryi type, four minesweepers, and 20 motor boats. Western intelligence feared that Nasser could have obtained the very dangerous Soviet submarines, as well as train appropriate personnel in the USSR and Poland[71].

Israeli navy was even smaller and consisted of two ex-British Z-type destroyers, a frigate, several armed boats and amphibious assault ship. Later, these forces would be strengthened.

In the Israeli nomenclature Israel's part in the operation "Musketeer" was code-named operation "Kadesh". In the initial phase of assault six infantry, two mechanized and one armoured were to take part. Also one parachute was to be dropped in the Sinai, with a possible option to invade Suez. Israeli Air Force was to play an important role there, neutralizing Egypt aviation over Sinai and preventing its strikes again the own land troops. This focused on three roads vulnerable to air raids: the first from Gaza Rafah and El-Arish to El-Qantara, the second from Beersheba via Abu Agheila and Bir Jifjafa to Ismaili and the third the hardest one form Kunitila via Themed, Nakhla and Mitla Pass to Suez.

The Egyptians had one infantry division between Gaza and Rafah, one in El-Arish and Abu Agheila, one in Bir Jifjafa and two west of Mitla Pass. Egyptian divisions, however, were less mobile and not suitable for highly mobile battlefield.

Participation of Israeli forces in the conflict began on 29 October 1956[72], when several DH Mosquito PR.16 rerre aircraft covered by modern Mystere fighters and archaic P-51D Mustangs performed several reconnaissance sorties deep in the Sinai and over the Canal. At about 14.00 hrs a group of 6 Mustangs of 116th Squadron flew into the Sinai with the task of breaking telegraph lines by gunfire, the cables hung from the fuselage or even propellers (!). About an hour later, 16 transport C-47 and Noratlas aircraft carrying paratrops of the 202nd Airborne Brigade took off. They were escorted by several Meteor F.Mk.8 fighters. About 17.00 hrs this formation flew over the Mitla Pass, where the paratroops were dropped. The same night, another group of transports brought 9 jeeps, 4 recoilless guns cal. 106 mm,

[71] M. H. Coles, *SUEZ 1956 A Successful Naval Operation Compromised by inept Political Leadership*, in: "Naval War College Review," Autumn 2006, Vol. 59, No. 4, p. 106 and R. Henriques, *A Hundred Hours to Suez: The Epic Story of Israel's Smashing Victory in the First Sinai Campaign*, ed. Pyramid Books, New York, 1957, pp. 19, 43, 180–181.

[72] As early as in the night on 28 October an Israeli Meteor NF.13 shot down over the Mediterranean an Egyptian Ilyushin Il-14 transport aircraft, which was carrying government delegation returning from Syria, where an alliance between Egypt, Syria and Jordan had been agreed. See R. Ball, *Israeli Air Force…*, p. 45.

two mortars cal. 120 mm and ammunition for the paratroops. The Israelis won had now a force 200 km deep into the territory still controlled by the Egyptians. The Egyptian side failed to react ion time. Headquarters in Cairo for a long time could not understand the intentions on advancing Israeli troops. When Israeli paratroops were digging in, the Egyptians sent against them three brigades from Suez. Three divisions deployed along the border with Israel held on to their positions, even when the Israeli mechanized divisions were bypassing them and penetrated 40 km behind Egyptian lines.

In the morning on October 30 the Israelis completed a provisional airfield at Mitla for light aircraft. Shortly after dusk the first three Piper Cubs landed there escorted by Mystere fighters from 101st Squadron. Around 07.30 hrs the first Egyptian fighters reached the Sinai, and their pilots had reported movements of the Israeli troops. It was decided to attack them with the entire potential Egypt had available. First, two MiG-15s attacked Israeli airfield at Mitla, destroying a Piper Cub. Then the MiG-15s attacked a column of the 202nd Brigade in the vicinity of Al-Thamed, destroying at least six vehicles. Other two MiG-15s shot down a Piper Cub over the Sinai. Approximately at 11.00 hrs four Egyptian Vampires raided anIsraeli column near al-Thamed, inflicting heavy losses. Then this column was attacked the Meteors of 5th Squadron escorted by MiG-15s, which aggravated the situation of 202nd Brigade.

The high losses inflicted by the Egyptian air force prompted the Israelis to take remedial steps. A total of 37 Ouragan, Mystere IV A and Meteor aircraft were sent to the air this morning and attacked Egyptian positions, especially the units heading toward the Mitla Pass. Around 15.30 hrs some Israeli planes took on six Egyptian MiG-15 and two Meteors F.Mk.8, which had took off from Kirbit. Egyptian fighters forced the Israelis to retreat, and then attacked the Israeli paratroops on the ground. The situation of Israeli troops became very dangerous. The reinforcement columns were fired at from the air and stuck in the soft sand.

Israeli Air Force intensified patrols over the Sinai. At approximately 16.00 hrs six Mysteres clashed with several MiG-17s in the vicinity of Kibrit. The Israelis surprised the Egyptians during the ascent and one MiG was shot down, but after one Mystere had been damaged they withdrew. However it diverted the attention of Egyptian fighters from Israeli bombers – this time the Ouragans destroyed many Egyptian vehicles of the 2nd Brigade, which enabled the Israeli paratroops of the 202nd Brigade to capture Mitla in the late afternoon. In retaliation the Egyptian Il-28s performed a few night raids on Israeli airfields at Tel Nov, Eilat and Ramat Rachel. It is not known whether they inflicted heavy losses (which is denied by Israel), and one of the bombers piloted by Sqn. Ldr. Hilmi crashed due to technical or navigational error. The sorties were prepared with assistance of the Soviets and Czechoslovaks, but then they did not take an active part in the fighting.

The Israeli army had done its job in the operation. It managed to take defensive positions about 80 km from Suez, which became the official pretext for Britain and France to issue ultimatum for both parties of the conflict to withdrew their troops to a distance of at least 20 km from the Canal. It was clear that the ultimatum would not be met by any of the parties. Otherwise, armed intervention of western forces might have been expected. Then, the Egyptian President Nasser realized why the British and French had formed so substantial naval force off the coast of Egypt.

In the morning on 31 October the fighting intensified. Egyptian destroyer Ibrahim Al-Awal shelled Haifa, but was counter-attacked by the French destroyer Kersaint and Israeli Yaffi and Eilat destroyers. Egyptian ship retreated and headed for Port Said but was bombed by Israeli fighter jets Ouragan. A Dacota, was marking the target by dropping flares. Egyptian crew surrendered and I. Al-Awal was towed by the Israelis to Haifa. In the meantime, two Ourgans and Meteors of 117th Squadron raided El-Arish airbase, hitting however, a number of well-prepared dummy planes.

On the ground, attack of Israeli troops at Abu Agheila was repulsed by Egyptian 3rd Division. Israeli attack on fortified positions at omm-Kattef also failed. At that time, Commanding Officer of the 202nd Brigade Col. Sharon ordered (contrary to the instructions of his superiors) a totally unnecessary attack from Mitla westwards. It had an aiur support, however, Israeli aircraft supported only the 7th Armoured Brigadem while the paratroops were left without any air cover. They were attacked by Egyptian Vampires and suffered heavy losses. Only then intervened the Israeli Mystere aircraft, which shot down three Vampires and damaged another. After this clash the Egyptians withdrew Vampires from fighter missions, because they were no match for Israeli jet fighters.

The fighter combats had revealed that Israeli Mysteres had greater power, greater fire rate and training of their pilots was much better than the Egyptian one. The Soviets were commencing deliveries of more MiG-15s and MiG-17s to Egypt. At approximately 08.00 hrs the Israelis discovered the Egyptian 1st Armoured Brigade, which was on the way to strengthen the positions at Bir Jifjafa. The Israeli Air Force intervened by sending against them four Harvard trainers of 140th Squadron. One of them was shot down, and the other crashed due to pilot's error. The second group of Harvards failed to find the target and two Meteors of 117th Squadron were damaged during attack at omm-Kattef.

At the same time the Egyptian 1st Armoured Brigade was attacked by Mustangs of 116th Squadron, which destroyed 6 tanks. Two P-51Ds were damaged. One of them was shot down on the way back by a MiG-15. Ataproximately 10.30 hrs a formationof seven MiG-17s attacked two Mysteres. Three of the MiGs began a dogfight with Lt. Yak Nevo, who managed to outmaneuver them and safely retreated. On their way back to the base the same two Mysteres met another two fighters of this type returning from a sortie to support the paratroops at the Mitla Pass (which came too late). The group of four Mysteres was then attacked by surprise by several MiGs. The Egyptians missed Israeli fighters, and one of their MiG-15s was damaged and forced to land in the shallow waters of the Sabkhet al-Bardawil lagoon. It was later found by the Israeli troops and transported to Israel, where it would be tested.

An hour later the Ouragans of 113th Squadron were on their way to bomb a number of targets between Bir Hasan and Jebel Libni, and they were attacked by several MiGs. Initially, the Israeli pilots identified them as their own Mysteres and did not take defensive steps. After a moment the MiGs opened fire, forcing the Israelis to flee and jettison all underwing equipment, including additional fuel tanks and unguided rocket launchers. One of the Ouragans was severely damaged by 23 mm cannon fire, and the second landed in the desert with no fuel. Later these MiGs shot down a Piper L-18 Super Cub observation plane over the Mitla Pass. Soon more of air combat will occur.

Two Mysteres clashed with several MiG-17s of 1st Squadron from Almaza, which were escorting the formation of Meteors of 5th Squadron attacking an Israeli column near Bir Hassan. Lt. Nevo shot down a MiG, the pilot catapulted when his MiG fell into a tailspin. His parachute did not open, but Egypt did not admit loss of any pilot on that day. The Meteors continued firing at the Israeli troops killing 27 soldiers, although a Meteor F. Mk.8 number 1424 was hit and must have landed. About 45 minutes later, at 13.30 hrs two Ouragans clashed with several MiG-15s over the Mitla Pass and this time Lt. Agasi damaged a MiG piloted by Flt. Lt. Farouke. Nevertheless, the MiG was able to fly safely back to Egypt.

In the afternoon, four Israeli Harvards performed another raid on the 1st Armoured Division, and this time did not suffer any losses. Around 14.00 hrs the 4 P-51D Mustangs of 105th Squadron dropped napalm bombs on Egyptian column in the vicinity of Bir Jifjafa, but lost one downed Mustang piloted by Lt. Paz who was forced to crash land in the desert. The Meteors of 117th Squadron bombed the 1st Armoured Brigade near the Abu Agheila, but four of them were hit on the way back and had to land in the desert. The 117th Squadron's attacks on Egyptian positions continued. 14 Israeli Mustangs were damaged. The commander of 105th Squadron in Maj. Tadmor was killed. The obsolete Mustangs still proved to be very effective in the ground attack role. In the evening on 31 October a Mosquito of 110th Squadron, piloted by Lt. Ash was severely damaged by anti-aircraft fire.

In the evening on 31 October the Israeli Air Force made 150 sorties over Sinai, of which 48 were made by the Ouragans and 30 by Meteors. Despite the losses, the Israelis managed to stop the Egyptian columns from taking advanced positions along the border, and troops defending the Abu Agheila were cut off from their rear. But at Mitla the Israeli troops were nailed by the Egyptians, who supported their troops with MiG-15;s, Meteors and Vampires as well as older Spitfires and Sea Furys. On that day the Egyptians made more than 100 sorties, and the morale of their aircraft crews increased. Although they did not manage to shoot down more Israeli aircraft in the air, they were very efficient in supporting their ground forces. The Egyptian pilots showed good coordination with the troops, good discipline and Israeli inflicted heavy losses to the Israelis. On the night of 1 November several Ilyushin Il-28 bombers (including some manned by pilots from the USSR) tried to bomb the Israeli Hatzor airbase, but the bombs missed the target. Situation on the land battlefield varied. In late afternoon on 31 October the 27th Israeli Mechanised Brigade assaulted the Egyptian positions at Gazah and Egyptian resistance in the northern Sinai began to fall. Within hours, the Egyptian troops that had been fighting with dedication for two days, scattered in the desert, often abandoning their weapons. The Israeli troops were in pursuit towards the west and north, having captured a lot of equipment left behind by the Egyptians. In the meantime, the conflict had been joined by France and Great Britain. Egypt was under a total assault.

Initially, the British and French were to commence bombing on 31 October at about 04.45 hrs, but it was postponed in order to first perform a series of reconnaissance flights, designed to indicate the current state of air forces of Egypt (especially the number of the operational MiGs). For this purpose, during the day four British Canberras and seven French RF-84Fs flied over at high altitudes over Egypt and were taking photos... On this basis the RAF experts agreed that Egypt had more than 110 ready to fly MiG-15s, 14 Meteors, 44 Vampires and 28 Il-28 bombers in the following bases: Abu Swayr (35 MiG-15s), Kibrit (31 MiG-15s), Inchas (20 MiG-15s), Almaza (25 MiG-15s/MiG-17s, 4 Meteors, 21 Vampires, 10 Il-28s), Fayd (9 Meteors, 12 Vampires), Cairo West (9 Vampires, 16 IL-28s), Luxor (22 Il-28s) and Kasfareet (1 Meteor and 2 Vampires).

The Egyptians sent some fighters to intercept the western reconnaissance aircraft, but they would not succeed. There was only one unresolved clash with a single RF-84F, the pilot of which after he had noticed a gunfire shot at him aborted his mission and returned to Cyprus.

The actions of the French and the British, however, were disrupted by the American operation "Cover", which was to evacuate American citizens from Egypt and Israel. The British tried to avoid the risk of accidental firing at the US planes that had landed in Egypt (at the Cairo West airport). It caused considerable congestion at airports in Cyprus and RAF was prompted to transfer the Meteor FR.9s from Akrotiri back to Malta.

The massed air offensive began in the evening, 31 October. The first Valiant bombers of 148th RAF Squadron took off from Malta on 17.20 hrs, but they were returned when at the Cairo West (which was to be their target) a US plane had been spotted. Eleven Canberras were also redirected from their route to Cairo West and sent to bomb Almaza. Another group of eleven Canberras from Cyprus and five Valiants plus seven Canberras from Malta took off to strike Kibrit. The third wave of the raid consisted of 18 Canberras from Cyprus and Malta, which were to attack Abu Swayr and 17 Canberras, which was sent over Inchas. In total, some 100 British bombers began their missions opening operation "Musketeer."

The Canberras of 139 RAF Squadron approximately at 21.30 hrs first appeared over their target – the Egyptian airbase in Almaza. The Airport West at Cairo was still fully illuminated, so finding it did not pose any problem. Seven Canberra of 10, 15, 44 and 139 Squadrons dropped 41 bombs, 454 kg each. Their crews reported the hangars and several transport aircraft had been hit. Nevertheless, later it turned out the actual damage was symbolic. A few minutes later, the first Valiants reached Almaza and dropped bombs on the runways. At this point the Egyptian fighters intervened. The British had been identified by the Egyptian radar system (which as we could see above, was not able to detect British bombers early enough), and three Egyptian Meteor NF.13s of 10th Squadron took off to intercept them. One of Meteors, support supported by the ground radar bearings found itself in good position behind a Valiant bomber. The Valiant had to make sharp maneuvers.

After the raid on Cairo West and another failure over Almaza, seven Canberra bombers dropped 132 bombs weighing 454 kg on Kibrit. The British crews again reported numerous targets hit, including Egyptian fighters, but the actual effects of the raid were not as good. Accuracy proved insufficient, which had something to do with the altitude they had not been trained for. The problem was also strong wind that pushed away the falling bombs. The crews then asked for an increase in altitude to avoid Egyptian fighters, and to stand in a calmer air layer, which would allow more precise aiming. Later, about midnight the next wave of bombers struck again at Abu Swayr and Inchas. They were intercepted by the Egyptian Meteors. One of them managed to fire at one Canberra, but the bomber outmaneuvred it.

Egypt's President Nasser personally watched the bombing from the balcony of his residence in Almaza. Then he had made a controversial decision – the Egyptian aviation should stop (!) intercepting British bombers. He stated that the raids of the western countries would not last too long and Egypt should save its strength for a confrontation with Israel. Perhaps he also had taken into account miserable effects of the first British air raids at Egyptian airbases and hoped for not too big losses because of that. Nasser also seemed to be aware that the vast majority of his pilots had not been trained adequately enough to face the world's elite – RAF and the French air force. But attacking the Israeli ground troops, the Egyptian aviation was quite effective. He decided to spare their pilots and let western aircraft in the Egyptian airspace. However, an order to evacuate aircraft to the airbases in southern Egypt or abroad was not issued, which in effect caused numerous losses of the Egyptian air force on the ground. As a result, from 1 November, EAF were virtually grounded and awaiting destruction. The Egyptian army felt it immediately and had to withdraw from fortified positions along the border with Israel and concentrate in the area of Suez Canal. In the morning, November 1st Egyptian aviation made only few sorties over the Sinai. Four MiG-17s of 1st Squadron commanded by Sqn. Ldr. Al-Hinnawi again raided positions of the 202nd Brigade in Mitla and knocked out several vehicles.

At that time, a group of two reconnaissance Canberra PR.7s and several RF-84Fs was on its way to Egypt with the task of photographing the effects of night raids. Pictures revealed that the Egyptian air force did suffer almost no losses. Despite the ban from the president, the Canberras were intercepted by the MiGs and one was damaged. The British crews were shocked, because they considered their planes impossible to be intercepted the outdated Egyptian air defense system.

Around 05.00 hrs the first British and French fighter-bombers took off from Cyprus with the task of destroying the Egyptian aircraft on the ground. 15 minutes later the British aircraft carriers HMS Eagle, HMS Albion and HMS Bulwark operating about 90 km from Alexandria also released their fighters. Since the United Kingdom and Egypt had used in some cases the same types of aircraft, the western coalition sported white "invasion stripes". The seaborne aircraft attacked the naval base east of Cairo, and aircraft operating from the airfields raided the Egyptian bases west of the capital city.

Despite the night air strikes, the first attacks next morning surprised the Egyptians completely. Only a few MiG-15s attempted to intercept the reconnaissance Canberras. Western aircraft (Venom, F-84F, Sea Hawk, Sea Venom, Wyvern) i subsequent raids inflicted on Egypt increasing losses. Approximately at 06.00 rows and rows of the aircraft parked at Kasfareet and Kibrit airbaseswere destroyed. A few minutes later, 16 Sea Hawk fighter aircraft from HMS Eagle struck Inchas. 12 Sea Hawks of HMS Bulwark bombed Cairo Airport West and Sea Venoms of HMS Albion struck Almaza airfield. Much attention was paid in order not to damage any US aircraft (especially at Cairo West), if any still survived. At pproximately 08.45 RAF and the French completed 58 soirties on Abu Swayr, Faridan, Kibrit, Fayd, Kasfareet and Almaza. Another wave of air strikes arrived between 09.30 and 13.30, having destroyed planes, hangars, shops and warehouses. British naval aviation (FAA) also bombed the airbases at Deklia and Cairo West.

Within a few hours 40% of the Egyptian military aviation had been annihilated. The Egyptian pilots were frustrated. Still they were forbidden to fight the British (the ban was at times broken), and often they were not allowed to evacuate their machines to safer airfields.. They could only watch as another Egyptian aircraft (including modern MiGs) explode under British and French bombs. The third wave of raids lasted from 13.30 to 17.00 hrs and consisted of 187 combat missions made by RAF and the French from Cyprus and 200 missions from British aircraft carriers.

This time the bombing was extremely precise. At Almaza alone the FAA pilots reported destruction of at least 22 MiG-15s, which was confirmed by the photographic evidence from Canberra PR.7s and RF-84Fs. The Egyptians responded with a long delay, only in the evening they evacuated first aircraft to airfields in the Nile Delta, south of Egypt, as well as to Syria and Saudi Arabia. At least 100 Egyptian aircraft were destroyed at the airfields on that day.

In the night some Il-28s were evacuated to Syria. One of them, manned by the Soviets, was intercepted by an Israeli Meteor NF.13, which erroneously identified it as a British Canberra and did not open fire. The Soviets reported that they had been intercepted by ten fighters, of which two were probably damaged by the tail gunners... So the Soviets say.

There was no fighting between Egyptian and British or French aircraft in the air. On 1 November the Anglo-French coalition actions however were disrupted by the Americans. At least twice American FJ3 Fury fighters approached the British aircraft carriers, having forced their fighter planes to take off and disrupting air traffic in the vicinity of ships. Some US commanders even asked for permission to attack the British and French, which reflected the state of relations between Europe and the US at that time[73].

Massive raids convinced the government of Egypt, that the Anglo-French invasion was imminent. The withdrawal of troops from the Sinai was ordered as well as sending more ground troops to the area of Port Said. Egyptian troops who had been retreating in haste without air cover suffered huge losses from Israeli raids. Most Egyptian troops was evacuated along the road from Al-Arish on the coast, where they were harassed by Israeli Mustangs. Only one P-51D was shot down and the pilot was rescued.

In addition, the French contingent that had been stationed in Israel also came into action. French fighter jets F-84F and Mystere performed 62 sorties that day, reporting the destruction of 34 T-34 tanks. None of the Frenchmen was not shot down, although few machines suffered damage. Two crashed on landing. The Israeli aircraft attacked Mitla, Bir Salim and Bir Jifjafa and to prevent the Egyptian troops toforma second line of defense. In the afternoon, the Israeli 27th Mechanized Brigade captured Al-Arish, along with stores of ammunition, 20 T-34 tanks, 6 SU-100 self-propelled guns and two Mraz light aircraft.

The next night the RAF repeated the series of raids atCairo West, Fayd, Kasfareet and Luxor airfields with Valiant and Canberra bombers. The Canberras of 15th Squadron were intended to destroy the 4 Il-28s at Luxor, as well as the runways. In the morning of 2 November the Egyptian air forces virtually no longer existed. Among these machines that survived most had been broken down. The rest of operational Egyptian MiG-15s, along with a few Il-28 and a number of Syrian MiG-15s stationing in Egypt in order to train Syrian pilots left Egypt.

---

[73]   T. Cooper, *Suez Crisis...*

Anglo-French command decided to begin the second phase of the operation "Musketeer", which was to cut off supplies to the Egyptian bases and weaken morale. First a raid of 18 Canberra bombers Canberra of 27, 44 and 61 Squadrons from Nicosia, escorted by 12 French F-84Fs at a radio station in Cairo was performed. The bombs were dropped from 1,000 metres and accurately hit the building with the main antenna mast. Over the next two days on the frequency of the destroyed radio station the British aired a propaganda program call,ed Radio Al-Adna. On the same day again the airfields at Almaza and Cairo were bombed, as well as the Egyptian army base nearby and huge stores in Huckstep. The US Navy continued to be active, a pair of RAF Venom fighters which was supposed to attack Kibrit was even intercepted by two American F9F8 fighter from VA-94 of the USS Randolph aircraft carrier.

At sea, the French Corsairs and Avengers sank an Egyptian patrol boat and almost clashed with two American destroyers in the vicinity of Alexandria. British Sea Hawk and Sea Venom fighters of the FAA repeated raids at Cairo West, Bilbeis, Dekhlia, Inchas and Almaza. Egyptian anti-aircraft defense was pretty poor, although one of Sea Venoms of the NAS 893 was hit over Almaza and its pilot Lt. Cdr. Willcox made an emergency landing on the deck of HMS Eagle. Later, the primary target of that day were stores in Huckstep bombarded by RAF Venoms, French F-84Fs and naval aviation. Despite the heavy anti-aircraft fire they were able to destroy hundreds of tanks and other vehicles. Lack of activity of Egyptian fighters caused that the older aircraft also saw action – the Wyverns and Corsairs (one was shot down by fire from Dekhlia, and its pilot Lt. Neve was rescued by a SAR helicopter).

On 2 November in the Sinai, the Israeli 37th Brigade attacked Omm-Kattef, supported from the air by the Mustangs. Then this unit accidentally clash with the Israeli 7th Armoured Brigade, which was mistakenly identified as the Egyptian troops. At that time, the Israeli Air Force focused on operations in the southern Sinai and supported the 9th Brigade which was to capture Sharm El-Sheikh and open the Straits of Tiran for shipping. Sharm El-Sheikh, however, turned out to be an extremely tough nut to crack. During one of the raids the Mystere piloted by Maj. Peled was shot down. He was rescued in the night by an L-18 (PA-18?). This target was also attacked by the older aircraft, such as Mosquitos, P-51D Mustangs and the Boeing B-17s. Several other Israeli planes were badly damaged. Perhaps the raids were premature because the Israeli 9th Brigade which was moving on the curved and narrow roads could get there only two days later. The Israelis, however, were keen to get the target quickly and did not abstain actions. Approximately at 17.00hrs a transport C-47 of 103th Squadron dropped two companies of paratroops (a total of 175 men) at a small village A-Tur south of Port Said. In the evening they built a provisional runway, where the planes with supplies needed for the offensive toward Sharm Al-Sheikh could land.

On the night of 3 November RAF sent 22 Canberra bombers from Cyprus for another raid at the airfield atLuxor, which caused a lot of losses. Successive waves of Canberras and Valiants bombed the airfield at Huckstep, before the weather forced the British to cancelall operations. The Egyptian losses were catastrophic and one of the main commanders of the army, Colonel Salim advised the president Nasser to commit suicide. Nevertheless, he supported the president when making important decisions (perhaps he consoled himself with false reports about the alleged successes on the Israeli front). Britain and France experienced a number of pressures from various parts of the world to stop the bombing. So they had to disconcert to do as much as possible in the shortest time. On 3 November 20 Canberras of 10, 15 and 44 Squadrons escorted by Hunter fighters, performed bombing of the railway stations in Nfisha and Ismail and the Almaza military base. The Egyptian air force did not react. Merely sporadic flights were made inorder to evacuate the aircraft to a safe place. Even such flights were not quite safe for the Egyptians. For example, close to Fayd a RAF Venom fighter destroyed two Egyptian Meteors, which had been refuelled. At the Kibrit airfield fighters of 6 Squadron RAF destroyed a MiG-15. Four other Venoms of the same unit performed a reccemission at low altitude near the Al-Qantara, where one of them (piloted by Flt. Lt. Sheehah) was shot down by Egyptian anti-aircraft artillery.

Fleet of the western coalition was then very active. HMS Albion moved away from the first line to be resupplied before the invasion. The other two British and two French aircraft carriers were to intensify operations to fill the gap. French Avenger bombers from the Arromanches aircraft carrier detected an American submarine USS Cutlass between the French ships and forced her to surface.

Aircraft from HMS Eagle were ordered to destroy a bridge in Gamil, located west of the airfield. To perform this mission several Sea Venoms and Wyverns took off, but failed to find the target. At this time, 8 Sea Hawks of HMS Bulwark struck Almaza and destroyed one Meteor, a transport C-46 and a T-6 Harvard trainer. French Corsairs attacked the airfield at Almaza, where Lt. de Lancrenon observed two Egyptian Meteors during takeoff. They avoided to engage. So Lancrenon decided to catch up with Egyptian fighters and shoot them, but was shot down himself by anti-aircraft fire. The fate of the French airman has not been known to this day. Radio Cairo reported that his Corsair crashed on the outskirts of Cairo, and the pilot was killed instantly. In turn, an Italian attache claimed that the Frenchman could have been killed by an angry mob. During this attack the Egyptians also damaged another Corsair. Another aircraft of this type landed on the LaFayette with a bomb, which did not fell off from under the wing and another Corsair almost did not manage to return to the aircraft carrier due to engine problems.

During the attack at the bridge in Gamil also a Wyvern piloted by Lt. McCarthy was hit. The Briton was able to fly over the sea and there he jumped off. Only recently it turned out that the formation of the Royal Navy aircraft was intercepted by two MiG-17s manned by the Soviets, led by Sergei Anatolyevich Sinkoy, who patrolled the area north of the Suez Canal. The aforementioned Wyvern was hit by him. Sinkoy had a damaged photo shoot camera, so he could not prove his victory. Bridge in Gamil finally collapsed after a direct hit of a 454 kg bomb during subsequent raids. In the evening Sea Hawks from HMS Bulwark several times bombed the airfield at Almaza, where 18 Chipmunk trainers and a number of Meteors, Harvards and even archaic Hawker Fury biplanes and Avro Lancaster bombers.

Since the Anglo-French operation had been continued, and the Soviets threatened with retaliation against Paris and London, the US government felt compelled to prepare for all eventualities. American Strategic Air Command (SAC) placed on standby the 306th Bomber Wing (BW), equipped with B-47 bombers and stationed in Morocco. On 26 October to the base of Sidi Slimane in Morocco additional B-47s of the 70th Strategic Reconnaissance Wing (SRW), in order to perform reconnaissance flights over Cyprus and Egypt. Several times they were intercepted by the RAF Hunters. Fighters fromthe the USS Coral Sea and USS Randolph were increasingly approaching the British and French fleet, which resulted in takeoffs of British aircraft (Sea Hawks or Sea Venoms). This forced the British to deploy naval reconnaissance and long-range patrol Avro Shackleton Mk. 2s of 37 Squadron at bases in Malta and in Libya. Their task was to survey the US aircraft carriers.

The Americans also used the anti-submarine E-1 Tracker aircraft, which sought British and French submarines to the south of Cyprus. Tension reached its peak when in the evening of 3 November the Israeli aircraft attacked a British destroyer in the vicinity of Sharm El-Sheikh (probably taking her for Egyptian vessel). This event in the worst case could lead to the disintegration of the Anglo-French-Israeli alliance. Britain demanded withdrawal of Israeli officers from the combined HQ centre, and suggested a possibility to attack Israel as well. Anything like that did not happen though.

After a while HMS Eagle and two French aircraft carriers were withdrawn in order to resupply. Analysis revealed that 158 of 216 Egyptian combat aircraft had been destroyed so far. The fighters of HMS Bulwark and HMS Albion were still making at least 355 sorties a day, bombarding columns and bases of the Egyptian army, especially Huckstep. They attacked several Egyptian patrol boats. Meanwhile, the American force led by the aircraft carrier USS Coral Sea began to operate in the same area as the the RoyalNavy. Despite the presence of numerous ships and aircraft (British and American), there were no collisions, either in the air or at sea.

RAF Venom fighter jets continued to bomb Egyptian airfields, claiming the destruction of 5 MiG-15s at Abu Swayr, while the French F-84Fs bombarded radar stations with unguided missiles. There were also raids on various targets in the area of Port Said.

Since the Egyptian air force had no longer been able to fight, and the situation in the Sinai was under control, the commander of French troops in Israel Cdt. Perseval asked for permission to bomb the airfield at Luxor, where there were the last Il-28 bombers. Approval was granted, and about 06.00 hrs 13 F-84Fs of theEC.1 led by Perseval himself took off to perform this task. They completely surprised the Egyptians, reporting that at least 20 Il-28s parked in rows were hit. The French were firing at everything that was at the airfield, inflicting heavy losses to the Egyptians. Five hours later, six F-84Fs again appeared over Luxor to complete the job. Then a reconnaissance RF-84F of the ER.4/33 based in Cyprus photographed the effects of strikes. A total of 17 Egyptian aircraft were destroyed, including at least 10 Il-28s. The only surviving Il-28 was then ferried by a pilot – Usama "Bunny" Sidki – to Jeddah in Saudi Arabia.

At that time, the Israeli army was busy with operations against the Sharm El-Sheikh. At noon, 5 Mustangs attacked the town with napalm bombs, which probably resulted in evacuation of the Egyptians on a few small vessels. Egyptian garrison surrendered the next morning as a result of further Israeli air strikes and assault of the paratroops. The Israelis taken prisoner 834 Egyptian soldiers. The rest of the Egyptian troops withdrew to the Canal area. The Israeli operation in the Sinai was completed.

Still ongoing, however, were bombing operations of the Western forces. On the night of 4 to 5 November the RAF Valiant and Canberra bombers appeared again over Egypt. This time their objectives were located far away from the intended landing areas, to distract the enemy. 19 bombers struck the artillery positions in the vicinity of Al-Agami, while 22 other bombers hit Huckstep and destroyed huge stockpiles of military equipment.

At the same time, the invasion fleet approached closer to Port Said and began disembarkment of equipment at 07.00 hrs. 18 transport aircraft Vickers Valetta of 30 and 33 Squadrons and 6 of 114 Squadron dropped 600 paratroops of the 3 Para/16th Brigade, who only days earlier had fought against the Greek insurgents in Cyprus. Their first target in Egypt was Gamil airfield in the area of Port Said. Drop of the paras was preceded by massive raid of the Venoms of 249 Squadron on the Egyptian positions in the area. Similar raids were made against the Huckstep airfield and paratroops were covered from the air by the latest RAF fighters Hawker Hunter. The Egyptians offered determined resistance on the ground, and two RAF fighters were damaged. At 07.15 "C" Company of 3 Para was already on the ground and in the next few minutes took control tower and the surrounding buildings. "B" Company captured the eastern part of the airfield, along with the buildings and the runway. From that moment on the paratroops were also supported by gunfire of the British and French ships. However, they could not approach too close to the coastline because of the presence of mins. Resistance against the paras was minimal,. The British lost only one of them, who had been dropped on the minefield.

The situation changed when some time later in the area arrived the Egyptian SU-100 self-propelled guns. But they were forced to withdraw by the continuous attacks of the French Corsairs. Subsequent raids destroyed many Egyptian vehicles and cleared the area of the Egyptian troops.

In the morning the French Avengers were sent to bomb the Egyptian fleet off Port Said, but they were forced to retreat by a strong anti-aircraft defence after just one bomb had been dropped. Another factor was the presence of American fighters FJ4 Fury behind them.

Approximately 09.00 hrs the Gamil airfield was secured. A few minutes later Whirlwind helicopters from HMS Eagle landed, bringing supplies and evacuating the wounded. At the same time, the Venom fighters from Akrotiri attacked Egyptian anti-aircraft artillery positions in the area, other fighters attacked an Egyptian column moving towards Gamil, 16 Canberra bombers struck Huckstep again. The Egyptians damaged three British planes, but none was shot down. About 13.00 hrs the paratroops in Gamil were surrounded by the Egyptian army battalion and two battalions of the Egyptian National Guard, including two units of the SU-100 guns. But the constant air support caused that in the next 45 minutes the British were able to land additional 100 paratroops, 7 jeeps with 106 mm recoiless guns and ammunition.

At that time, the British and French naval aircraft continued to raid Almaza, where a number of MiGs and one Il-28 had been sighted. They were destroyed. Here, too, they encountered the heavy anti-aircraft fire. One of the Egyptian guns was firing from the rooftop of the hospital. The pilots tried not to hit civilian targets by performing low-level attacks at a short distance from the target. One Wyvern fighter shot down during the attack on the Egyptian coast guard base. The pilot managed to bail out and was rescued by a Whirlwind helicopter from HMS Eagle.

Despite the problems, around noon on 5 November the paratroops broke out of their drop zone. After some time, they captured more Egyptian positions, having inflicted heavy losses. In the evening, Port Said was already cut off from the rest of Egypt. Egyptians lost probably over 200 killed and wounded, while the British losses amounted to 4 killed and 36 wounded. In the evening, the situation in Gamil was already so stable that the French C-47 transports landed there. Egyptian commander at Port Said was considering surrender and Radio Cairo reported on the alleged start of World War III and the Soviet troops were approaching to Egypt. It turned out untrue, of course.

Like the British, also the Frenchmade use of their paratroops. French Nord Noratlas transport aircraft of the ET.1/61 and ET.3/61 escorted by F-84Fs dropped 500 paratroopers of the 2nd RPC (colonial parachute unit) over bridges at Al-Raswa. Despite the loss of two soldiers, the western bridge was quickly secured, and Corsair aircraft of the 14F and 15F squadrons performed a series of strikes on Egyptian troops having destroyed several SU-100s. The F-84Fs also hit large fuel depots in Port Said, which went up in flames and covered most of the city with a thick layer of smoke that would last for several days. In the evening extra 552 paratroops were dropped near Port Fuad. French Corsairs still intensely provided support from the air. The aircraft from the LaFayette made at least 40 sorties, which ended after sunset (although the pilots did not have permission for night flights). The French lost a total of 10 killed and 30 wounded during the landing and the fighting that followed shortly afterwards.

Egypt's President Nasser tried to obtain significant assistance from the Soviet Union, but the Soviets were then busy with intervention in Hungary and did not show much interest. Paradoxically, it is not the Soviet Union (as claimed by propaganda), but above all, the presence of US forces resulted in faster end of the conflict. The administration in Washington was keeping pressure on London and Paris and warned the Soviet Union that, in the event of the involvement of Soviet forces in the conflict, the Americans will defend the British and French[74].

On the night of 5/6 November the invasion fleet approached finally the coast of Egypt. The French battleship Jean Bart, a French cruiser Georges Leygues and British cruisers HMS Ceylon and HMS Jamaica began shelling the Egyptian coastal batteries, but only with the rounds of smaller calibre than 114 mm to minimize losses among civilian objects.

Shortly after dawn the Venom fighters of 249 Squadron RAF also attacked the Egyptian artillery positions and appeared over Port Said at the same time, when a single MiG-15 performed the only Egyptian air attack against British paratroops in Gamil. British pilot Fl. Of. Budd immediately attacked the MiG, but it managed to escape, owing to a much higher speed than the Venoms. Around 05.45 the first commandos landed on the beaches at Port Said. Half an hour later the first Centurion tanks disembarked. The commandos together with tanks then moved through the city to the south.

At the same time, Whirlwind helicopters of the 845 NAS landed the commandos near the football stadium. A few minutes later they were surrounded by the Egyptians, and they were again evacuated by helicopters, one of which suffered at least 22 hits. Landings with helicopters were also performed in several other parts of the city. Over the next half an hour 6 Whirlwind HAR.2 and 6 Sycamore HC-14 helicopters of the Joint Helicopter Unit (JHU) and 7 Whirlwind HAR.2s of the 845 NAS landed 417 troops and 20 tons of equipment, evacuated the wounded (one of the injured on board of an aircraft carrier just 19 minutes after he had been picked up by the helicopter). Only one helicopter was lost. It was a Whitlwind of the 845 NAS, which ran out of fuel while having transported the wounded from HMS Eagle

---

[74]   T. Cooper, *Suez Crisis…*

to HMS Theseus, about 800 m from the latter. All those who were on board were rescued by another helicopter. One Sycamore of the JHU was also damaged during a hard landing on board of HMS Ocean.

After the commandos and Centurion tanks had joined the paratroops in Gamil, additional supplies was provided by the C-47 and Valetta aircraft. The Venom fighters and F-84Fs performed more strikes on the Egyptian positions in the area of Ismail, but soon the enemy resistance would become symbolic.

The naval aviation was, however, still very busy, mainly mopping up enemy forces facing the commandos and Centurion tanks, which were moving south.

Until approximately 10.00 hrs at least 70 sorties had been made. Egyptian anti-aircraft artillery continued to fire from time to time achieved some success. A Sea Hawk fighter of the 800 NAS flown by Lt. Stuart-Jervis was shot down. He bailed out at sea and was rescued (interestingly, this aviator in 1995 participated in the Gordon Benett Cup as a balloon pilot who was shot down over Belarus by a Mi-24. The entire crew was killed).

Shortly thereafter, over the road from Port Fuad to Ismaili a Sea Hawk of the 897 NAS piloted by Lt. Mills was shot down. Pilot bailed out and was rescued from the enemy-held territory by a Whirlwind helicopter, covered by other aircraft of the squadron. The Egyptian tanks were present nearby.

In the evening, the British commandos encountered the Egyptian troops' resistance south of Port Said, but the Sea Hawks made some efficient raids, after which the march continued. In the meantime, the rest of the 16th Brigade and Centurion tanks of the 6 RTR arrived on the beach and set off south. On the left side Suez the French 1e REF disembarked together with the marines and AMX-13 tanks of the 7th Division. These units were also sent to the south.

If the British and the French had more time, no doubt they would be able to occupy the entire area of the Canal. However, political pressure (mainly from the US) soon led to a ceasefire. The French then cancelled next landing of ground troops (paratroops of the 1e RCP) in Ismaili, and the British halted their paras and tanks at El-Cap. One Sea Hawk and two Whirlwinds were heavily damaged and had to be withdrawn from service.

One of the reasons for which the French and British agreed to a ceasefire had been American reports on allegedly almost 132 MiGs concentrated in Syria, which could have theoretically bombed the base in Cyprus. The British sent several reconnaissance Canberras over Syria to check the credibility of these reports. One of them was nearly intercepted by a Syrian Meteor F.Mk.8 piloted by Lt. Al-Assad. Two other Canberras performed recce mission over the Rayak airfield in Lebanon and over Aleppo in Syria. One of them was shot down by a Syrian Meteor. One member of the crew was killed and the other two managed to bail out and landed only a few meters away from the Syrian border in Lebanon (full description of the story can

be found in the D. Nicolle's publication ("Canberra Down"). All subsequent reconnaissance missions over Syria were carried out only with the fighter escort (British
Hunters or French F-84Fs).

The coalition aviaton was characterized by high morale, although there was a case
when a British airman intentionally damaged his Canberra after he had took off from
Malta in order not to participate in the bombing of Egypt[75]. Even before there was
an official ceasefire, the United Nations had begun to form a contingent of peace
that was to be sent to Egypt. On 15 November, the first UN troops reached Abu
Swayr on the Swissair DC-4 and DC-6 planes.

In the "Operation Musketeer" 80,000 troops, 550 aircraft from 5 different air bases
and 7 aircraft carriers, as well as 130 other ships were involved. From the military
point of view, it was a huge success for the western coalition. However, from a political point of view soon it would prove to be a complete failure.

The Israeli Air Force performed a total of 1,846 combat missions, of which at
least 831 by the archaic Piper Cub and Boeing (Stearman) PT-17 Kaydet aircraft.
Three Piper Cub aircraft were lost: one shot down by a MiG-15, one destroyed on
the ground and one crashed in Jordan. The Noratlas and C-47 transports performed
192 flights. The Mystere, Ouragan, Meteor and outdated P-51 Mustang fighters and
T-6 Harvards performed a total of 489 sorties. Nine Mustangs were lost, plus one
Mystere and two Harvards. Next five Mustangs were probably withdrawn because
of heavy damage. Two Meteors, one Ouragan, one Mystere and two Harvards were
damaged but repairable. Five Israeli pilots were killed and one was captured. Israeli
pilots reported having shot down 4 Vampires, 3 MiG-15s and 1 Il-14, as well as
the destruction of 22 tanks, 17 armoured vehicles and 260 other vehicles[76]. French
planes stationed in Israel made most likely about 100 sorties. The French lost two
F-84Fs in accidents.

Aviation of Egypt carried out at least 200 sorties against the Israeli troops. In
it lost three MiG-15s (including one captured by the Israeli troops), probably one
MiG-17, 4 Vampire FB.52s, 2 Meteors and 2 Mraz M.1 Sokol light aircraft (including
one captured by the Israelis). The Egyptians during the fighting in Sinai lost about
1,000 killed and 4,000 wounded soldiers and about 400 tanks and other vehicles.
Egypt air force showed high efficiency in attacking Israeli ground troops, but as we
know their actions against the Western coalition were a failure. The bombing by the
Western countries resulted in the complete destruction of the Egyptian Air Force,
but only 5 pilots and about 200 other members of the air force personnel were killed.
The air bases and radar sites were destroyed. Although the level of inflicted damage reported by Western pilots had been even double inflated, the losses of Egypt

---

[75] T. Cooper, *Suez Crisis...*
[76] *Ibidem.*

were enormous. The British later agreed that Egypt lost 104 MiG-15s/ MiG-17s, 26 Il-26s, 30 Vampires, 11 Meteors and 63 other aircraft (mainly trainers, but also the Sea Furys, Spitfires and a Lancaster). A further 50 were seriously damaged. It was also agreed that another 10 MiG-15s, 16 Il-28s, 4 Meteors, 14 Vampires, 6 Spitfire, 30 trainers, 31 transports and 22 other aircraft were slightly damaged or escaped to Syria and Saudi Arabia. These figures indicate that USSR probably delivered to Egypt 30 MiG-15s/MiG-17s between 29 October and 6 November 1956. As for the Egyptian ground troops' losses in the area of Port Said, the British estimatios were 650 killed and 900 wounded[77].

British and French aircraft performed more than 5,000 combat missions, including the most massive air raids since the Korean War. Canberra bombers operating from Malta performed 72 flights and the Valiants additional 49, having dropped a total of 1,439 bombs 454 kg each. Fighters from HMS Eagle performed 621 sorties, and from HMS Albion 415 flights. They dropped 72 454 kg bombs, 150 250 kg bombs, fired 1,448 unguided missiles and 88,000 30 mm rounds. 23 British airmen were killed and 96 wounded. 1 Canberra bomber was shot down (over Syria), 1 Venom, 2 Sea Hawks, 2 Wyverns and 2 Whirlwind helicopters. 50 British aircraft were damaged. France lost 10 killed and 33 wounded airmen and 1 Corsair fighter shot down. A few Corsairs and F-84Fs were damaged.

The most important lesson learned from this war was enormous role of the aircraft carriers, including ships equipped with helicopters which made possible swift landing and dropping large amounts of men and equipment in a short time. It is also recognized that the air defense fighters are not needed if one gets air supremacy by a sudden surprise attack on the enemy air force. The Canberra and Valiant bombers proved vulnerable to enemy fighters fire and not very effective in the strike missions. It was decided that they must be supplemented by fighter-bomber aircraft.

The French also drew right conclusions on the high efficiency of aircraft carriers in the expeditionary missions. They also noticed that their aircraft carriers were too small, and the aviation operates on the border of wear and tear, because obsolescence of Corsairs and Avengers. The French navy was obliged to acquire two new medium-sized aircraft carriers, which would be completed in the early 1960's. Also new generation of aircraft were ordered for them, which would in service until 1990's. The French had also realized that in the next conflict, the opponent could have aviation capable of the fleet's destruction, so soon they would purchase F-8 Crusader fighter jets.

The only participant of the conflict, which had emerged victorious in both the military and political ways was Israel. The armed forces under the sign of the Star of David demonstrated to the western powers its effectiveness and determination. Israel

---

[77] T. Cooper, *Suez Crisis…*

was then supplied with modern weapons, which meant that the Israeli armed forces (especially aviation) had become one of the more dangerous in the Middle East.

USA were not interested in further continuation of the conflict in the Middle East and the possible seizure of control over the Suez Canal, because it could cause escalation of the conflict in the region and incalculable results of it[78]. Washington appealed to the UN General Assembly proposing the adoption of a resolution calling for a ceasefire, withdrawal of troops and the opening of the Suez Canal for shipping. UN forced the British to withdraw of all forces from Egypt until 22 November 1956. Two weeks earlier, on 7 November withrawal of Canberra and Valiant bombers from Cyprus and Malta. Most of the units that had participated in the operation "Musketeer" returned home before Christmas. Although RAF 15, 61 and 109 Squadrons remained in Cyprus until 1957. Both the British and the French navies left the area between Cyprus and Egypt until 10 November. Just as the American fleet. Flight crews were overtired by weeks of intense fighting, which affected the safety of flights at a later date. Between 14 and 18 November one Sea Hawk crashed during landing, and one Sea Venom was destroyed in an accident in the hangar on HMS Eagle, which killed a mechanic. The French lost in accidents a Corsair from the Arromanches aircraft carrier and RF-84F from Akrotiri.

Paradoxically, defeated militarily Egypt had proven to be a political winner of this conflict[79]. After the withdrawal of western forces, it became clear that none of the European powers would ever return to Egypt in the way they had done in the past. Egypt has established extensive cooperation with the Soviet Union, which lasted for several years. Nasser, despite the military defeat, had become a hero for the Arab world. Around it began to crystallize the pan-Arab movement, which postulated liberation of all Arab countries out of control of the West. The decrease in the international significance of France and the UK as a result of the conflict accelerated the process of decolonization throughout the world. Egypt with the support of the United Nations once again took control of the Suez Canal, and Israel in accordance with UN Resolution left Sinai and the Gaza Strip in the spring, which came under the control of a temporary international peacekeeping force – UNEF. The overall effect of the conflict for the country, however, was in fact positive.

---

[78] President Eisenhower warned the UK that he would sell the US reserves of the sterling and thus cause the collapse of the British currency. In addition, Saudi Arabia announced an embargo on oil supplies to Britain and France, and the United States refused to fill the gaps in the supply of fuel until withdrawal of British and French troops from Egypt. As a result of these pressures on 6 November 1956 all military operations in Egypt stopped. Then, on 6 December Israel moved its troops to a distance of 30 km from the Suez Canal, and on 7 March 1957, Israel completed the withdrawal of its troops from the Sinai Peninsula and the Gaza Strip. K. Love, Suez: *The Twice-Fought War*, ed. McGraw Hill, New York 1969, p. 651 and D. Hill (ed.), *Kronika wojen, ed.* AKA, Głuchołazy 2009, p. 189.

[79] See: Corm G., *Le Proche-Orient eclate 1956–2000*, Gallimard 2010.

2.2. The Six Day War 1967

Israel declared independence on 14 May 1948. No Arab country recognized it, mainly because of ideological hostility to the Jewish people, and secondly due to the fact that an independent Palestine had not been created next to it (according to a decision of the UN former British protectorate of Palestine was to be divided into two independent states: Jewish and Palestinian). In fact, all the time fighting took place there of varying intensity, from local skirmishes to open war. Some of them have passed permanently into the history of the use of combat aircraft on the battlefield.

The first of these was a conflict, which took place in 1967 called "Six-Day War", when the Israeli armed forces due to mass and decisive strikes (mainly from the air) defeated Arab forces, having secured its independence. The basic strike force of Israel were the aircraft[80]. Preparations of the air force for such a conflict had lasted from 1953[81]. Dan Tolkowski, the IAF commanging officer commenced them by large-scale purchase of aviation equipment. Training programmes followed the RAF patterns with addition of own experiences. For example, due to appropriate training of technical personnel, the average time of restoration of combat readiness of anIsraeli aircraft from landing to another takeoff was 7–10 minutes (in the USA 20 minutes, in Egypt 3–4 hours)[82]. Thus Israeli pilots could perform up to eight missions per day for several days. For each aircraft there were at least three pilots.

In the development of its air force, Israel focused mainly on the multirole aircraft. Limited financial resources did not allow for the luxury of specialized aircraft – bombers or fighters. Israeli Air Force's doctrine assumed first the destruction of Arab aviation on the ground, and then, after reign in the air had been gained, support of own ground troops[83]. The multi-role aircraft were best suited for both tasks.

Gen. Tolkowski realized that the combined Arab forces would always have the numerical advantage. Israel oppose them with the predominance in quality. It was possible to achieve due to the higher level of civilization level of Israeli society, than in the Arab societies. Tolkowski gained the advantage due to constant and strictly followed training procedures. In contrast to many conscript Arab armies, the Israeli armed forces were the army of citizens.

The modern equipment had to be obtained. In the first years after independence, Israel was buying the equipment mainly from the communist countries, especially in the USSR and Czechoslovakia (the Czech copies of Messershmitt Bf-109G – Avia S-199). At the turn of the 50's and 60's it was no longer possible, however. West-

---

[80] E. Zabłocki, *Współczesne siły powietrzne*, ed. AON, Warsaw, 2002, p. 13.
[81] A. Radomyski, *Gorące niebo nad Bliskim Wschodem*, ed. Adam Marszałek, Toruń, 2007, p. 24.
[82] *Ibidem*, s. 24.
[83] E. Zabłocki, *Współczesne siły...*, p. 83.

ern countries have also been cautious in supplying weapons to the country. Israel, however, somewhat accidentally established friendly relations with France because of the common enemy (Egyptian President Nasser, who supported the Islamic insurgency in the French Algeria). In return for the support of Israel in the war of the Suez Canal in 1956[84] the French in 1957 built a nuclear reactor in Dimona on the Negev desert[85], which was very important for the Jewish state[86]. In the same year, the commander of the air force became gen. Ezer Weizman, an ex-RAF World War II pilot. He proposed operation "MOKED" which was to assume massive and rapid bombardment of almost all Arab airbases inorder toparalyze the United Arab Republic[87] aviation and other countries' in the region, which posed a theat to Israel. Several variants of this operation were developed[88]:

"MOKED" A – action against Egypt only

"MOKED" B – attack on Syria

"MOKED" C – attack on Egypt and Syria or Egypt, Syria and Jordan

"MOKED" D – attack on Egypt, Iraq, Jordan and Syria

The plan assumed that the majority of enemy airbases could be reached by the low altitude flights over the Mediterranean Sea, below the visibility level of Arab radars. A formation of 3–4 aircraft was to perform one flight to bomb and destroy runways, and then three raids in when the aircraft parked on the ground would be fired at with cannons[89]. As we can see, it had been assumed that it was enough to destroy them.

To conduct such an operation, however, the most modern aircraft were needed, as the older types (Ouragan, Mystere or Vantour) were too slow and losses among them could have been too heavy for Israel. Soon Israel acquired appropriate machines. These were 76 French Mirage IIICJ[90] ("J" for "juif", or Jewish in French). It was called the Shahak in Israel. The Mirage IIICJ had two DEFA 5–52 30 mm cannon (125 rounds) and three external underwing hardpoints with a capacity of 454 kg each. The aircraft was fitted with the Cyrano II radar and could carry short

---

[84]   J. Solarz, *Doktryny militarne XX wieku*, ed. Avalon, Kraków, 2009, p. 410–413.

[85]   The Americans were aware of the importance of this event and were recconnoitring the object with high-altitude U-2 spy planes. I. Rendall, *Splash one: The story of jet combat*, W&N publ. 1998.

[86]   S. Dunstan, *The Six Day War 1967: Sinai*, Osprey 2009.

[87]   United Arab Republic (UAR) – a quasi-state created on 1 February1958 from the merger of Egypt and Syria. On 5 February 1958 its president became Gamal Abdel Nasser. On 29 September 1961 in Syria there was a coup led by young officers, as a result of which Syria withdrew from the union. Egypt kept the name United Arab Republic until 1971. In addition, in 1958–1961 Egypt, Syria and Yemen formed a confederation under the name of United Arab States.

[88]   S. Dunstan, *The Six Day War 1967: Sinai*, Osprey 2009.

[89]   *Ibidem*.

[90]   Israel constantly needed the aircraft that could provide a technical balance to the Arab machines. When Egypt had acquired a supersonic fighter MiG-19, Israel bought Super Mystere B2, while the response to the Egyptian and Syrian MiG-21s, were French Mirage IIIs.

range air-to-air AIM-9 Sindewinder guided missiles and Matra R530[91] medium range missiles[92]. It reached a maximum speed of 2.2 Ma, the ceiling of 17,000 m and range of 1,350 km. Compared to previous machines, this was a technical revolution. In Israel a special rocket-engine bomb was developed to destroy runways. Mirage IIICJ had become the primary engine for planned variant of the operation "MOKED". The Israeli intelligence perfectly recognized the potential targets and provided current information about the Egyptian aircraft and pilots. The latest photos of Egyptian bases, taken by US SR-71 Blackbird spy planes were obtained on a daily basis[93]. In the Negev desert the mock Egyptian airfields were built, together with models of aircraft measuring about 1.5 m, which were constantly attacked during exercises. As a result of excellent preparations, combat readiness of the Israeli Air Force was 90% (of the Egyptian aircraft 30% only[94]). The Israeli pilots kept practicing also the very low altitude flights, to avoid detection by radar.

Israeli Air Force on 5 June 1967 constisted of the following aircraft[95]:

67 modern multi-role Mirage IIICJ/BJ/CJ(R) interceptors

35 Super Mystere B.2 fighters

35 Mystere IVA fighters

19 Vatour IIA/N/BR ground attack aircraft

51 Ouragan fighters

approx. 15 Meteor F.MK.8, FR.Mk.9 and T.Mk.7/8 fighters

1 Soviet MiG-21F13 fighter[96]

---

[91] The R.530 missile had a replaceable tracking warhead with infrared systems for short range attacks (only the rear hemisphere) and the semi-active radiolocation system for medium distances. R.530 was introduced in France in 1963. In the basic version R.530 could hit targets at 15 km, which then was classified as medium range. They proved to be ineffective. In 1967 probably a single enemy plane (Egyptian MiG-19) was shot down wit hit. This took place on 28 November and was the first case to hit an enemy aircraft with guided air-to-air missile in the history of IAF. It was fired by a Mirage III covering an archaic Piper Cub (!), which performed reconnaissance flight over the border with Egypt in the Sinai. Source: I. Rendall, *Splash one: The story of jet combat*, W&N publ. 1998. See also J. Grzegorzewski, Z. Skierski, *Nowoczesna broń lotnicza*, ed. MON, Warsaw, 1984, p. 227.

[92] B. Gunston, M. Spick, *Modern air combat*, ed. Salamander books, London, 1983, p. 94–95.

[93] The Americans had flown nine intelligence missions over Egypt, Jordan and Syria with SR-71 Blackbird aircraft of the 9thSRW (Strategic Reconnaisance Wing), which took off from the Griffis base near New York City. The route of the mission was longer than 19,300 km, and it took about 10 hours and 18 minutes to get over the target. In the meantime, the SR-71 to refuel five times in the air. Source: J. Gotowała, *Lotnictwo we współczesnych konfliktach zbrojnych 1945–2003*, ed. Bellona, Warsaw, 2004, *p*. 84.

[94] S. Dunstan, *The Six Day War 1967: Sinai*, Osprey 2009.

[95] A. Radomyski, *Gorące...*, p. 25.

[96] It was the plane on which the Iraqi pilot Munir Radf fled to Israel, 16 August 1966. This was due to Mossad action aimed at obtaining such an aircraft. The MiG-21F13 received then the Israeli markings, and during the Six Day War it acted as an emergency measure to repel any raid of Arab aircraft over the Israeli airspace. Currently, it is displayed at aviation museum in Hatzerim. In addition, during the Six Day War, Israel captured 6 Algerian MiG-21F13s, which were transferred to the US, where already in the USAF livery performed test flights as YF-110. Israel had also a certain amount of Soviet air-to-air missiles R-3S (AA-2 Atoll), which were captured in the Egyptian depot in Bir Gifgaf. They were fitted to the Mirage IIIs

As we can see, the Israeli Air Force boasted a total of 223 aircraft, of which only 67 were modern (Mirage III). In June 1967 197 of them were completely prepared for combat operations, but only 183 could be fully manned by crews[97].

The most powerful air force among the Arab states was the Egyptian aviation. The country had about 560 aircraft and military helicopters plus some reserve. There were 431 combat aircraft, including 278 fighters – MiG-15, MiG-17 (and probably Polish Lim-5[98]), MiG-19, MiG-21 and Su-7 figher-bombers, as well as 30 strategic bombers Tu-16[99] and Il-28 bombers. J. Gotowała[100] claims that the Arab coalition forces had a total of 730 aircraft (410 Egypt, Syria 200, Jordan 120), and Israel 400. Still other data is given by S. Dunstan[101] – Israel 286 (including 196 combat on the front), Egypt 431, Jordan 28, Syria 227 and Iraq 106. The air defense of Egypt was organized with the assistance of the Soviets and modelled on the Warsaw Pact pattern[102]. It was based on a strict ground control of all air defence means of. Fighters were not given permission to free hunting (as often happened in IAF), but only followed orders from ground control stations. Individual Egyptian pilots hadno or hardly no awareness of tactical situation on the battlefield (they knew mostly what they saw from their own cockpits) – everything had to be decided by the command post. Their task was to mechanically execute commands with virtually no invention of their own. The same system of command and organization of the air forces was introduced also in Syria and Iraq. Methods of training in the USSR and its allies had been widely studied by the Israeli intelligence services. For example, the Polish pilot Ryszard Obacz who in 1963 fled to the West on a TS-8 Bies, mentions that after the escape he was interrogated daily by intelligence officers from different countries, for which he got paid. He talked, among others, to Israeli officers who received the training programmes of Polish pilots[103].

In order to deceit the Arab states, Israel applied various stratagems. One of them was secret mobilization connected with sending vast numbers of soldiers on the beaches and thus make an impression that they were on long leaves. The Arabs

---

and used in combat. In the opinion of the Israeli pilots who used them, the old and rusty R-3Ss were equally ineffective, as the first Israeli missiles called Shafrir, which were still in the experimental stage. The first air-to-air missiles were inaccurate and had too weak warheads. It happened that the Israeli planes were able to return to base, despite having received a hit by a R-3S fired by Arab MiGs. Source: J. Spektor, *Loud and Clear: The Memoir of an Israeli Fighter Pilot*, Zenith Press 2009.

[97]   A. Radomyski, *Gorące...*, p. 26.
[98]   A. Zbiegniewski, *MiG-i z bazy...*, p. 42, 48.
[99]   A. Radomyski, *Gorące...*, p. 26.
[100]   J. Gotowała, *Lotnictwo we współczesnych konfliktach zbrojnych 1945–2003*, ed. Bellona, Warsaw, 2004, p. 84.
[101]   S. Dunstan, *The Six Day War 1967: Sinai*, Osprey 2009.
[102]   I. Rendall, *Splash one: The story...*
[103]   R. Kowal, *Rozmowy ze zdrajcą*, ed. Internovator, Warsaw, 1998, p. 59.

recognized that in the near future Israel would not be planning a military operation, but diplomatical measures[104] only.

The first raids on the Egyptian airports had been scheduled for 08.45 hrs Cairo time (07.45 Israeli time), most likely because of the following reasons[105]:
- On the basis of radar observations it had been found that between 07.00 and 08.00 hrs lesser number of Egyptian radar sites were active, when compared to other hours. Many stations were temporarily turned off for maintenance.
- Egyptian fighters on duty at night, inearly morning reacted to Israeli provocative flights, carried out almost daily. However, the Egyptians usually landed around 07.00 hrs and then for a few hours did not perform any sorties.
- Employees of the Egyptian state services (including the armed forces) started work at 09.00 hrs. Strike at 08.45 would find most of the officers only on their way to work or during training or briefing, but not at their battle stations.
- It had been noted that at this time over large areas of the Nile Delta and in the area of the Suez Canal were covered by the mist, through which one could secretly reach most Egyptian airbases.

Operations began on 5 June 1967 about 07.10 hrs[106], when 16 Fouga Magister trainers took off for routine patrol missions in order to confuse the enemy. They maintained radio frequencies typically used by pilots of the Mirages and Mysteres. Between 07.14 and 07.30 next 183 combat aircraft took off, which accounted for 95% of the Israeli military aviation. To defend Israel's territory, only 12 fighters had been left, including the only MiG-21F13.

After the takeoff, most of the machines headed west toward the Mediterranean. Interestingly, most of them were detected by Jordanian radars (British production). The Jordanians immediately sent a warning to Egypt, but it was not read because the previous day the Egyptians had changed their radio codes and did not inform the Jordanians.

After eighteen minutes of flight over the sea, the Israeli formation turned south, maintaining the total radio silence. Most likely, the Cyrano II radars of the Israeli Mirage IIICJs were also turned off all the time in order to not reveal their presence.

In Tel Aviv headquarters of the Air Force gathered in an underground command bunker in Kirji, waiting for news. The success of the war and the future of the State of Israel depended on the success of the operation "MOKED." The first wave of attack headed toward ten selected Egyptian air bases. Then was to come a strike at another fourteen airfields.

---

[104] *Ibidem*, s. 165.
[105] A. Radomyski, *Gorące...*, p. 30.
[106] S. Dunstan, *The Six Day War 1967: Sinai*, Osprey 2009.

The Israeli pilots were inadvertently helped by the commander of the Egyptian army, Marshal Abdel Hakim Amer himself, who at that time, accompanied by the commander of the Air Force General M. S. Mahmoud flew on an An-12 to inspect the troops in Sinai. The order was given to do not open fire at any aircraft on the Antonov's route[107]. As we can suspect, it had completely confused the anti-aircraft defense in the area.

Most of the Egyptian radar stations, which were then active, searched for a possible opponent in the east (towards Israel), meanwhile, the Israeli formation was approaching from the north. A short distance from the Egyptian air bases, the Israeli formation soared suddenly to 2,750 m to start bombing. Capt. Awihu Bin-Nun recalls these moments[108]: *When I dived and dropped the bombs, I saw four MiG-21s at the end of the runway, waiting in line to take off. I pulled the bomb trigger, opened fire and hit two of the four. Both burst into flames. When I looked up, I saw a huge transport plane Antonov-12 coming in for a landing in front of me. Pilot of the Antonov noticed the exploding MiGs and turned south. I was faced with the dilemma of whether I should shoot it down, or to continue the attack according to plan? Because I could not contact the formation and destruction of all MiGs at the airbase was of great importance, I decided to act as it had been scheduled. During the strike we destroyed 16 of the 40 aircraft on the ground, and then we paralyzed the SA-2 battery on our way back.*

The aforementioned An-12 was carrying Marshal Amer and Gen. Mahmoud, who miraculously escaped the downing. R. Ball says that Antonov was not destroyed, as the Israeli pilots had orders to fire at strictly combat aircraft, so they left the transport plane alone[109]. Paradoxically, eventually it would result in success because subsequent incompetent leaderhip of Amer only accelerated the Israeli victory[110].

Israeli aircraft were successfully destroying base after base. First the formations of 3–4 planes were dropping Durandal anti-concrete bombs (for the destruction of runways) or conventional bombs. Then, according to plan, they attacked aircraft parked on the ground. Within 20 minutes every base was attacked three times. Egyptian planes stood in rows, which made ideal conditions to destroy many of them during each of the raids[111]. In particular, efforts were made to destroy all 30

---

[107] *Ibidem.*

[108] *Ibidem*, p.33

[109] R. Ball, *The Israeli Air Force...*, p. 76.

[110] Ibid. Some sources indicate that the An-12 did not turn back, but landed at the Fayid air base, where it was hit on the ground. This seems unlikely, however, because all Egyptian commanders survived. See I. Rendall, *Splash one: The story...*

[111] The Egyptians made the same mistake as the Americans at Pearl Harbor in 1941. Setting the aircraft in formation at airbases, although helps to guard them against sabotage, but are easier to destroy in the air raid. After the experiences of Egypt during this conflict, the air forces around the world (including Polish), began to disperse aircraft at the airbases. Previously, setting machines in parade formation was very popular. Another effect of these experiences was repainting almost all Egyptian combat aircraft with camouflage colours (previously the majority sported the natural metallic colour). After the war in 1967 it

Tu-16 bombers[112], which could raze more than one Israeli city had they managed to take off and reach Israel[113].

They were all hit at the airbases. The second most important targets were modern MiG-21 fighters, equalling the performance of the Mirage IIIs, of which more than a hundred were in the Egyptian hands. Most of them were also eliminated. Next to be destroyed were MiG-19 fighters, subsonic MiG-17s (including Lim-5s) and MiG-15s and transport aircraft (eg. Il-14s and An-12s) as well as the helicopters (Mi-1s, Mi-4s or other).

Flights were performed at the lowest altitude to visually identify targets and to distinguish them from possible mockups. The pilots had been instructed to keep a reserve of 1/3 of the fuel and the same amount of cannon ammunition in case a dogfight in the air should occur[114]. But only a few Egyptian fighters managed to get in the air.

At 0800 hrs Israeli time (09.00 in Cairo), two bases in Egypt and two in the Sinai were completely destroyed. The first wave of air strikes lasted 80 minutes. Then, after 10 minutes, there was another wave which lasted another 80 minutes. During these 170 minutes, Egypt lost 293 aircraft: 30 Tu-16 strategic bombers (all that had been at disposal), 27 Il-28 medium-range bombers, 12 Su-7 fighter-bombers, 90 MiG-21 fighters, 20 MiG-19 fighters, 75 subsonic MiG-17 fighters (including Lim-5) and more than 30 transport aircraft, trainers and helicopters[115]. Many Egyptian aircraft that had attempted to land at the bombed runways crashed or did not land anywhere, hovering in the air until the fuel was exhausted. Some Egyptian planes landed at civilian airport in Cairo. They were hit on the ground there, although the plan had not assumed attacking civilian airports[116].

---

had been done in such a hurry, for example, that part of the MiG-17 fighters were hastily repainted with paints seized at a nearby car manufacturer!

[112] All Tu-16 bombers had been stationed at the Cairo-West airbase, so it was a priority target. See S. Aloni, *Arab-Israeli air wars from 1947 to 1982*, ed. Osprey, Great Britain 2001, p. 29.

[113] The Tupolev Tu-16 bomber (NATO code: Badger) was the most dangerous weapon in the arsenals of Egypt and Iraq, capable to destroy many targets in Israel. Tu-16 could speed at maximum 1,050 km/h, cruising at 850 km h, ceiling of 12,300 m, radius of action 3,150 km. Its armament consisted of 7 AM-23 23mm cannons and bomb load up to 9,000 kg, including the air-to-ship missiles (or air-to-ground) Raduga KS-1 Kometa (AS-1 Kennel by the Tu-16KS) and newer Raduga KSR-2 (AS-5 Kelt), including anti-radar version CRS-11 guided with passive radar 2PRG-11. Egypt received the first several dozen (30?), Tu-16s armed with KS-1 missiles in the spring of 1967. Probably they were all destroyed on the first day of the Six Day War. After this conflict Egyptians rebuilt their fleet with Tu-16Ts, Tu-16R reconnaissance aircraft and Tu-16KSR-2-11 missile carriers (with KSR-2 missiles). At a time the Soviet Union strongly encouraged Poland to get these machines, but this has never happened because of the huge cost of maintenance. See also: C. Chant, *Wielkie bombowce świata*, ed. Bellona, Warsaw, 2002, pp. 150–153 and J. Grzegorzewski, *Samolot bombowy Tu-16*, ed. Bellona, Warsaw 2000, pp. 13–14, 19–20 and 30–31.

[114] S. Dunstan, *The Six Day War 1967: Sinai*, Osprey 2009.

[115] *Ibidem*

[116] I. Rednall, *Bandyci na...*, p. 159.

Israel lost ten aircraft during the strikes: 3 Super Mysteres, 2 Mysteres, 4 Ouragans and 1 Fouga Magister. Six other were heavily damaged. Six airmen were killed, including one mistakenly shot down by the Israeli Hawk missile battery[117].

When the Egyptian armed forces had been in agony the Soviet Union very seriously took into consideration the raids of Soviet Tu-95 strategic bombers at targets in Israel to relieve the Arab ally. Several Tu-95 were even hastily repainted with Egyptian markings[118].

About 12.45 hrs the Israeli aviation shifted its efforts on Syria and Jordan. Within 30 minutes they made 52 sorties against Jordan, destroying all of its 28 combat aircraft. Syria lost 57 machines, which accounted for 2/3 of its air force. There was also a raid on the Iraqi H3 airfield, where 10 aircraft were destroyed[119]. The remainder were evacuated deep into Iraq.

Aviation of the Arab countries hardly managed to carry out retaliatory strikes. Iraq reportedly sent one of its six Tu-16 bombers over Tel Aviv (huge damage could have been made), but it was shot down. The Egyptians could no longer do anything after the first blows. On a limited scale the aircraft from Syria and Iraq attempted to react, but they did not achieve any success, and after a few hours of fighting, their air bases were also destroyed. The air was dominated only by the aircraft with the Star of David.

It is also worth noting that Israeli pilots had learned how to destroy the Lavochkin S-75 (SA-2 Guideline) missile batteries[120], and in particular their guidance stations. This was done in the following way[121]:

1. Approach at altitude of 50–70 m.
2. At a distance of 3–5 km ahead of target, the attacker went up to 1,200–1,500 m and dived to bomb the target.
3. Then again performed flight at low altitude and re-appeared over the target to engage it from 50–70 m with unguided missiles and cannons.

---

[117] S. Dunstan, *The Six Day War 1967: Sinai*, Osprey 2009.

[118] V. Ryeshentikov, *Na kursie bojowym*, ed. L&L, Gdańsk, 2008, pp. 349–352.

[119] Some sources claim that Iraq lost 12 MiG-21F13s and MiG-21PFs alone Iraq. Soon, these losses would be complemented by the supply of new MiG-21PFMs from the Soviet Union. See P. Przymusiała, *MiG-21 na świecie*, Pt. 3, in: "Aeroplan" Issue No. 4/1996.

[120] Egypt was the first Arab user of the S-75 sets. The first such systems were imported from the Soviet Union to Egypt in 1965 while in 1968–1969 a certain amount of S-75M2 sets plus W-750WN missiles and radiolocation stations RSNA-75M. Since 1973 Egypt was also buying the 20DSU missiles. Egyptian industry sought to develop (in cooperation with North Korea and France), its own variant of the W-750W, named Ta`ir al Sabah. The modernized missile was to have a greater range, to be more accurate and to reduce the dependence of Egypt on supplies from the Soviet Union. This programme, however, was cancelled. See: A. Radomyski, *Gorące niebo...*, pp. 147–148.

[121] *Ibidem*, p. 43.

Until, dusk on June 6, the Israeli air force destroyed 416 Arab aircraft, including 393 on the ground[122]. At the same time, Israel lost 26 planes shot down mainly by the anti-aircraft defense. Having dominated in the air, the Israeli Air Force effortlessly attacked the Egyptian army.

Operation "MOKED" was a complete success and amazed the world. The Israeli Air Force now had complete control in the air, which gave them the opportunity to support their own land troops, which fought against the Egyptian army in the Sinai. For example, when Israeli tanks had blocked the Mitla Pass in the Sinai, the Egyptian army was trapped. By the end of the war the Israeli Air Force destroyed there 700 tanks, 520 guns, more than 12,000 lorries. 10,000–12,000 soldiers were killed, and 5,500 were taken prisoner[123]. The Egyptian Su-7s tried to help their colleagues of the land forces and raided the Israeli troops, but were not able to inflict significant losses. By the end of the war, Israeli aircraft destroyed a total of approximately 450 enemy aircraft[124], for a loss of 46 own machines[125] and 20 airmen[126].

This gives a final score of 10:1. In fact, the war had been won already in the first three hours[127], when the Israeli Air Force eliminated the Egyptian airbases and most of the combat aircraft of that state. The subsequent defeat of Egypt, after the loss of dominance in the air, was only a matter of time. On 10 June at 18.30 hrs a truce was announced. On 12 June the Israeli troops occupied strategic positions on Mount Hermon, which is considered the last act of war in the conflict.

The Arab pilots often fought bravely (especially the Egyptians), but were unable to oppose the perfect strategy of Israel. The Jewish state won the territory two and a half times larger than its original area[128] and regained a strategic buffer zone – the Sinai. The Suez Canal had been then closed to shipping and Israeli Gen. Chaim Bar-Lev ordered to build a network of fortifications on its bank, known as the Bar-Lev Line. The Egyptians dug in on the opposite bank.

It is also worth noting that in this conflict the Arab armies (especially Egyptian), were not technically inferior to Israel, and sometimes even exceed it (the Tu-16 bombers, a large number of modern MiG-21 fighters, the S-75 air defense systems[129]

---

[122] *Ibidem.*

[123] I.Randall, *Bandyci na...*, p. 166.

[124] I. Rendall says that of this number, 60 Arab planes were shot down in the air and exclusively by a gunfire. According to this author, none of the Israeli air-to-air missiles hit the target. See I. Rendall, *Splash one: The story...*

[125] Egyptian AA defence downed 44 aircraft, including 35 by artillery and only 9 by missiles. Source: A. Radomyski, *Gorące...*, p. 46.

[126] *Ibidem.*

[127] *Ibidem*, p. 43.

[128] I. Rendall, *Splash one: The story...*

[129] In 1967 Egypt had 18 batteries of S-75s. During this conflict, they fired only 22 W-750WK missiles, having downed two Mirage IIIs (7 and 8 June). During the operations, the Israeli Air Force destroyed eight of these batteries, and one was captured by the Israeli army. Along with 12 W-750WK missiles and

etc.). The decisive factors proved to be the excellent preparation on the Israeli side and basically complete lack of preparation on the Arab side. It was the same as far as the land forces were concerned.

So successful air raid the world had not seen since the attack on Pearl Harbor in 1941. Operation "MOKED" has become a perfect example, where the outcome of war had been decided by air strikes in the first few hours of the conflict. Ironically, it was Israel in 1967 that demonstrated a perfect example of "Blitzkrieg", even more efficient than German operations in Poland and France during World War II.

Israel achieved all crucial military goals, but none of the political objectives. This conflict even deepened the political divisions, because the reluctance of the Arab world had increased. The consequence was another conflict, which Israel and the Arab world fought and still have been fighting to date. Without operation "MOKED", and hence, the Arab forces' defeat in the Six Day War, the days of Israel would have probably be numbered. Israel was therefore forced to do so.

Israel was not a member of NATO, so did not apply the doctrine adopted by NATO. Commanders of the IDF developed their own theory of "Blitzkrieg", based on the experience of earlier conflicts, including World War II. It was assumed that the victory over the air forces of the Arab countries must have been achieved in a sudden way, which was a reference to the views of the Germans during World War II, having taken into account new technologies and new jet powered aircraft. In turn, the then doctrine of NATO and the Warsaw Pact did not provide for the escalation of local conflicts conducted by their allies to the level of a nuclear war. Therefore, none of the parties of the conflict did not get this kind of support from the US or the Soviet Union, the Soviets even decided to cancel the conventional bombing of targets in Israel with their Tu-95 strategic bombers.

Just as in the Korean War, the risk of escalation of the conflict to the level of nuclear war because it was too high. At that time it had been already realized the threat of the outbreak of total nuclear war (the theory of mutual destruction – MAD), when victory would not have been achieved by any of the parties – there would be only the mutual destruction of both sides.

One has to admit, however, that the conflict has become a kind of example of what Douhet had wanted – the victory was almost exclusively won by the air forces, which effectively had defeated the armed forces and vital centres of the enemy.

---

the radar the latter was later transferred to the US, where it undoubtedly proved invaluable in later research on fighting the S-75s in Vietnam. Source: A. Radomyski, *Gorące...*, p. 46

Air Combat of the Air Forces of Israel since 1956

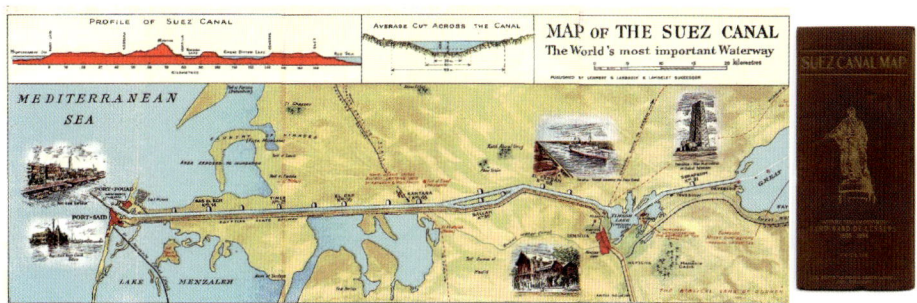

The Suez Canal in 1920's

The President Nasser greeted by the Egyptians shortly after the Suez Canal had been nationalized

The Israeli Mystere IVA jet fighters

The British paras about to board a Shackleton transport aircraft, Cyprus, 1956

The evacuated British women and children at home again. A Handley Page Hermes of the Britavia airlines, Blackbush, 1956. When the air strikes over Egypt commenced, there had been still still about 1,000 UK subjects and 10,000 from the colonies, not evacuated.
470 of them were repressed. The HM Government was then heavily criticized for having failed to evacuate all the citizens

British Vickers Valiant bomber

The Westland Wyvern fighter aircraft

The Israeli Gloster Meteor fighters on display at the Hatzerim Museum (in the foreground a two-seater radar equipped NF.13 night fighter variant).

Hawker Sea Hawk FGA.6, 899 Squadron, taking off HMS Eagle

Three cheers to the Piper Cub

5 November 1956. Port Side after it had been raided by British aircraft

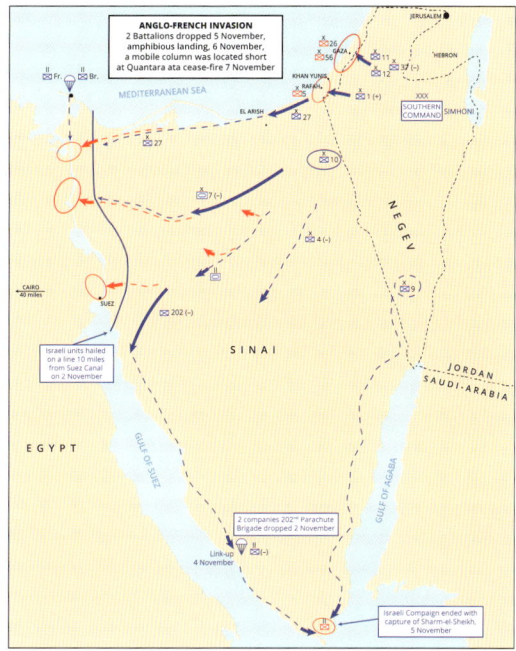

The Suez Canal Campaign as seen by the Department of History, U.S. Military Academy

A damaged Sea Venom on board of HMS Eagle

Egyptian Soviet manufactured SU-100 assault gun in Cairo

Vought Corsair assault aircraft in the French livery

Another Vought Corsair aboard the French aircraft carrier

French Vought Corsair about to take off

Egyptian MiG-15 which had been downed by an Israeli Mystere, but managed to crash-land on Bardavil Lake where it was captured by the Israeli troops

Three Egyptian MiG-17s at Almaza air base sout-east of Cairo. In the background the MiG-15 fighters can be seen (or perhaps their Polish copies – the WSK Lim-5s). Note the original national identity markings. They had been sported before the UARAF (The United Arab Republic Air Force) was formedon Bardavil Lake where it was captured by the Israeli troops

Egyptian Il-28 bombing the Israeli positions

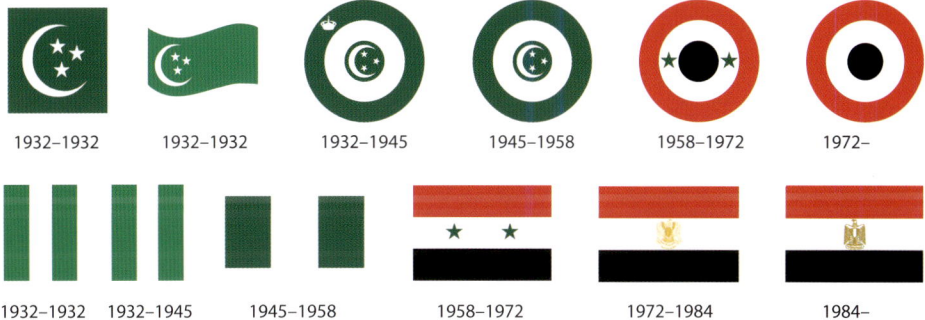

1932–1932   1932–1932   1932–1945   1945–1958   1958–1972   1972–

1932–1932   1932–1945   1945–1958   1958–1972   1972–1984   1984–

The Egyptian national identity markings from 1932 to date

Egyptian MiG-15bis after it had
crash-landed

Egyptian Gloster Meteor T.7

The battlefield – seems like a photomontage

The Israeli Gloster Meteors

A Whirlwind helicopter landing on board of HMS Theseus

The Westland Whirlwind and Bristol Sycamore helicopters aboard HMS Theseus. In the background a French hospital vessel can be seen

Israeli P-51D Mustang, Operation „Kadesh".
On the left side under a cockpit a marking can
be seen which denotes the Egyptian telephone
cables had been cut off

Israeli De Havilland Mosquito

Israeli P-51D Mustang

The Sea Hawk F.1 fighters about to take off from HMS Eagle

American FJ3 fighter jet aboard the USS Forrestal, 1956

British reconnaissance Canberra PR.7 WH799 aircraft, 1956

The Six Day War 1967

The IAF Super Mystere B.2, 105th Squadron taking off at the Hator air base

Another Super Mystere of the 105th Squadron, IAF

Mirage IIIA. The kill sign denotes downed Jordanian aircraft

Israeli
Mirage III

The Israeli Mirage III with markings of three Arab aircraft (two Iraqi and one Libyan) shoot
down by this IAF pilot – the chief of staff Yitzhak Rabin

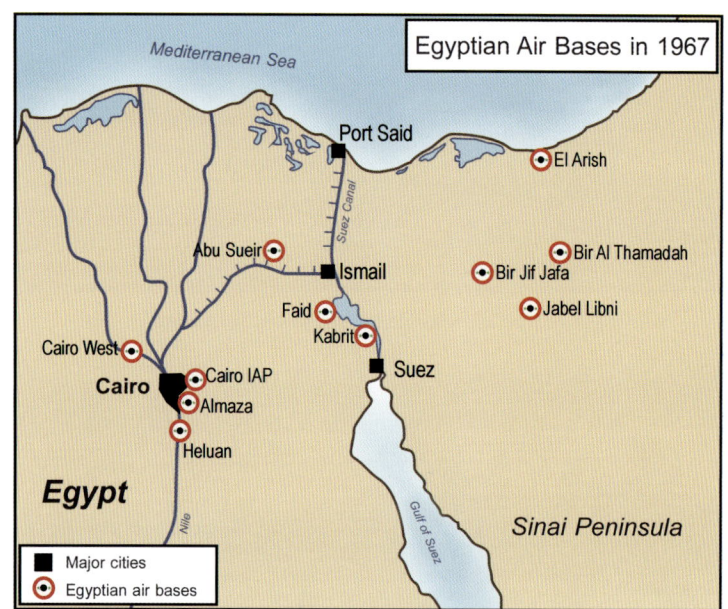

Egyptian air bases in 1967

Syrian air bases, June 1967

Egyptian MiG-21PFM

The Algerian MiG-21F13 fighters having assisted the Egyptians

Syrian MiG-17F, which mistakenly landed at Israeli airfield

Syrian MiG-17F, which mistakenly landed at Israeli airfield

Now on display at the IAF Museum, Hatzerim

Egyptian MiG-17F

Wreckage of an Egyptian MiG-17F. The El-Arish air base

Egyptian Il-14 transport aircraft destroyed at the airbase

The Lavotschkin S-75 (SA-2 Guideline) surface-to-air system

R530 air-to-air missile under the Israeli Mirage III

Painted by Janusz Świątłoń

Egyptian MiG-17PF of the 31st Squadron, 12th Aviation Regiment, Kabrit airbase, June 1967

Egyptian MiG-17F No. 2335 of the 18th Squadron, 12th Aviation Regiment, at the El Arish air base in Sinai, June 1967. The aircraft was field-modified to carry bombs (racks on both sides of the fuselage) and the underwing Sakr 76 mm missiles

Egyptian MiG-17F No. 2647 of the 18th Squadron, 12th Aviation Regiment, June 1967. Black stripes around the back of the fuselage and wing tips denote the EAF front-line aircraft and had been applied since the 1950's

Egyptian MiG-17F No. 2975, the early 70's. Shortly after the Six Day War the Egyptian Air Force began to paint its combat aircraft with camouflage colours. The aircraft sports new national identity markings introduced after the collapse of the United Arab Republic in 1971

Egyptian Tu-16 at the airbase

Egyptian Tu-16

The underwing air-to-surface/sea Raduga KSR-2 (AS-5 Kelt) missile and the Egyptian Tu-16

Isareli Vautour bomber making a low pass over the Israeli Centurion tank column

The IAF Sud Ouest Aviation (SNCASO) S.O. 4050 Vautour II

Sud Ouest S.O. 4050 Vautour IIB

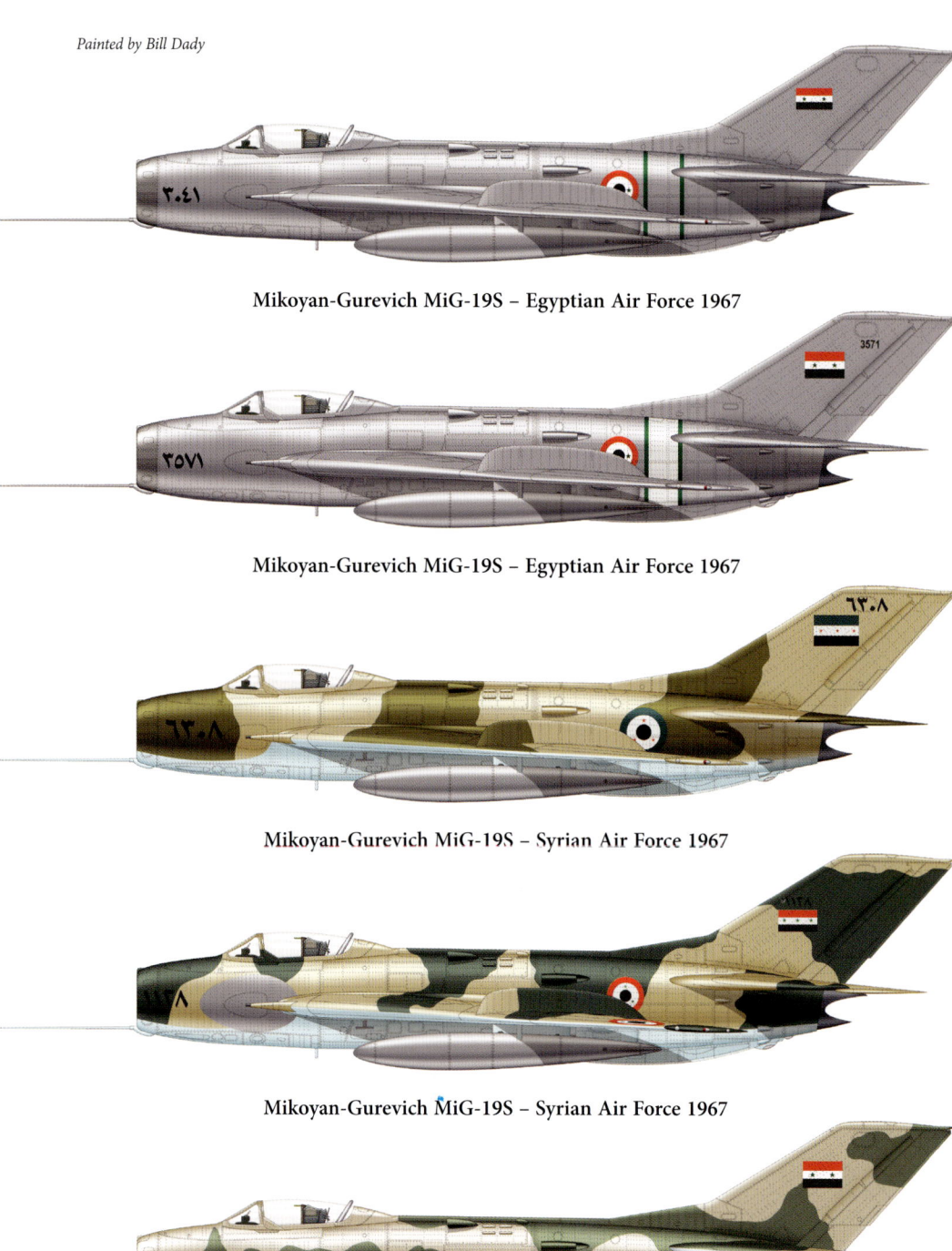

Mikoyan-Gurevich MiG-19S – Egyptian Air Force 1967

Mikoyan-Gurevich MiG-19S – Egyptian Air Force 1967

Mikoyan-Gurevich MiG-19S – Syrian Air Force 1967

Mikoyan-Gurevich MiG-19S – Syrian Air Force 1967

Mikoyan-Gurevich MiG-19S – Egyptian Air Force 1968. That MiG-19 has R-3S (AA-2) missiles
under wings, which were very rarely used for this type of aircraft

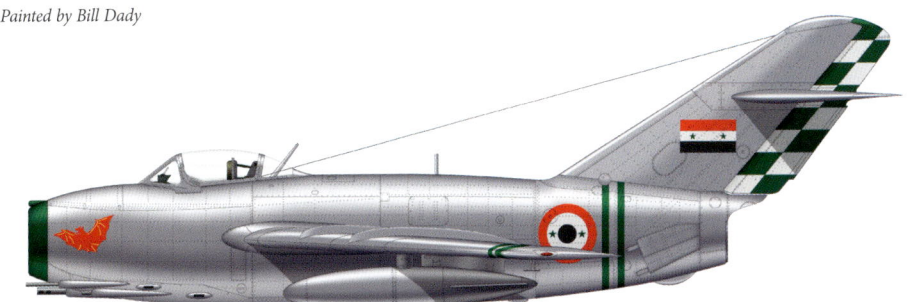

Mikoyan-Gurevich MiG-15 bis – Egyptian (UAR) Air Force 1965

Mikoyan-Gurevich MiG-15 UTI – Egyptian (UAR) Air Force 1967

Mikoyan-Gurevich MiG-17F – Egyptian Air Force 1967

Mikoyan-Gurevich MiG-17F – Egyptian Air Force 1967

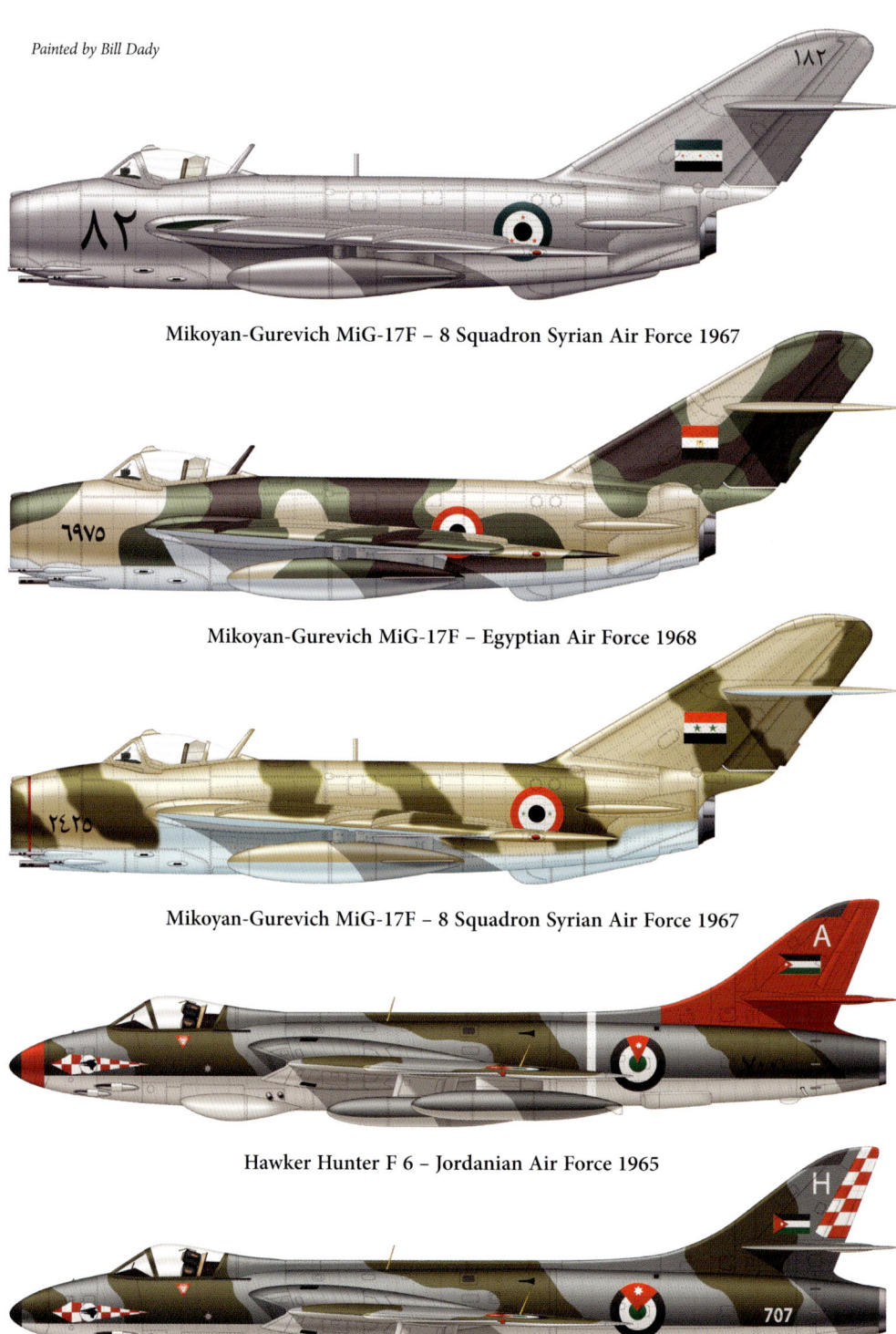

Painted by Bill Dady

Mikoyan-Gurevich MiG-17F – 8 Squadron Syrian Air Force 1967

Mikoyan-Gurevich MiG-17F – Egyptian Air Force 1968

Mikoyan-Gurevich MiG-17F – 8 Squadron Syrian Air Force 1967

Hawker Hunter F 6 – Jordanian Air Force 1965

Hawker Hunter F 6 – Jordanian Air Force 1967

2.3. Yom Kippur War of 1973

The end of the Six Day War had not brought peace to the region of the Middle East. The Arab states, despite enormous losses, did not intend to recognize Israel's existence. None of the parties of the conflict do not even want to join the major international agreement plans with the opposing state. Even if between Israel and the Arab states something had been signed, it would be usually done under the external influence (UN, USA and the USSR), and the agreements proved to be not sustainable. The Israeli government came to the conclusion that due to inability of establishing any permanent political principles, the status quo in the region had to be maintained by the military. Soon, Israeli troops fortified the recently occupied positions in the Sinai peninsula (the Suez Canal), against Egypt and in the area of the Golan Heights against Syria. An important buffer line had been thus created, which moved the areas of potential fighting further from the centres of the Israeli population (afterwards Israel would break this rule by creating a number of settlements in the vicinity of the borders).

Despite the formal end of the Six Day War, a cycle of the limited range clashes continued. All kinds of armed forces of Israel were harassing the Arab states, but the major role was played by aviation again. The Israeli aircraft attacked almost everyday the missile launcher sites, radar stations, communication centres and other selected military facilities. It had provided the Israeli pilots not only a large dose of combat experience, but also knowledge of new types of weapons and new methods applied by the opponents.

Retaliatory raids on Israeli targets in the Sinai was also performed by Egyptian air force[130]. For example, on 24 January 1970 the Egyptians bombed El Arish[131]. The Arab operations, however, could not be compared with Israel's action as far as the scale was concerned.

That war of attrition generated enormous costs for both sides. Both Israel and the Arab states quietly sought other solutions to this problem. Egypt in the early 70's was not yet ready for open full-scale military confrontation because it needed time to re-arm and re-train the armed forces. Jordan was busy with internal problems (the conflict with radical Palestinian groups). For Israel, the hardest to accept was continuous loss of life, especially because of the limited demographic potential of the country.

Under pressure from the United States, on 7 August 1970 the cease-fire between Israel, Egypt and Jordan was signed[132]. It was the first and last peaceful diplomatic

---

[130] C. Starface, *Arab air forces, ed.* Squadron-Signal, Texas, USA, 1994, p. 14.
[131] J. Biziewski, K. Kubiak, *Jom Kippur, ed.* Altair, Warsaw, 1995, p. 5.
[132] *Ibidem*, p. 6

success of that era in the region. However, it was short-lived. Shortly afterwards the Middle East was heading towards war again..

In September 1971 the Federation of Arab Republics was proclaimed. It was formed by Egypt, Libya and Syria. The high commands of Egyptian and Syrian armed forces soon began to prepare a joint operation against Israel.

At this time, Israel found itself in partial international isolation. As a result of the Six Day War, France put an arms and spare parts embargo, which significantly hindered the logistics of the Israeli armed forces, especially aviation and navy. The crisis was resolved only after production of military equipment had started in Israel, and as a result of vast supplies of weapons from the United States.

The plans of the Arab leaders for the future joint international operation assumed clearing almost entire Sinai of Israeli troops (to the Sinai Mountains) and recover lost Syrian territories[133].

In the meantime, both sides carried out extensive work on the modernization and training of their forces. The Israeli command realized that for the second time they could not count for the same surprise as in 1967. They knew, however, that this time the Arabs could attack unexpectedly. Therefore, Israeli Air Force began construction of numerous underground hangars and depots. The strengthened hangars were built in large quantities, which could withstand all but direct hit by a heavy bomb.

During the Six Day War the modern French Mirage IIICJ fighter had performed very well. Even before the Israeli Air Force had cooperated with Dassault in the design of the Mirage 5J, capable to achieve 2.2 Ma speed (upgrade of the Mirage III). Israel ordered 50 such machines and paid for them[134]. However, immediately after the conflict France, having had some common interests with the Arabic world[135], cancelled the supplies of arms to Israel. Not only that, in exchange for oil, France began to arm the Arab states. Paradoxically, the substantial numbers of the Israeli Mirage 5Js were exported to Egypt and Libya! For Israel, it was a blow and caused even more caution and application "limited confidence" principle against the world powers. At that time, Israel established secret relations with the racist government of South Africa, which also had been isolated in the international scene. South Africa also had managed to acquire the Mirage III fighter jets, before the embargo was put. In the meantime, the Israeli intelligence service was able to steal the plans of Mirage 5 in France and Switzerland[136]. In co-operation with the South African industry, Israel was thus capable to develop its own copy of the aircraft – the IAI Nesher.

---

[133] *Ibidem.*

[134] I. Rendall, *Splash one: The story...*

[135] Egypt supported the fight against the Islamic extremists in French-occupied Algeria. Hence, Egypt and France had a common enemy. In addition, France was purchasing large quantities of Arab oil.

[136] I. Rendall, *Splash one: The story...*

USSR dynamically re-armed the Arab armed forces. The priority was given to aviation and antiaircraft systems. Next to the older S-75 (SA-2) the supplies of the modern Isayev S-125 Neva (SA-3 Goa) commenced. The latter was capable to hit targets at altitude of 100 m[137]. The Striela (SA-7 Grail) MANPADS and ZSU-23-4 vehicles armed with four 23 mm guns had been delivered, too. It was a very dangerous weapon. The aim of Soviet advisers was to create an integrated air defense system modelled on the one of the Soviet Union and the Warsaw Pact. Just like in Vietnam, most antiaircraft systems (especially the S-125s) were manned by the Soviet crews. Alongside the entire Suez Canal antiaircraft missile and gun sites had been located. Until mid 1968 Egypt had regained its air force potential from before the Six Day War[138]. The quick pace of re-arming the Arab states by the Soviet Union meant that the United States decided to lift the embargo and to commence weapon deliveries to Israel. The first American jets supplied to Israel were 48 Douglas A-4 Skyhawk assault aircraft, which had been delivered in late 1967 and entered service a year later. Israel acquired a total of 300 of these machines[139].

The air war of attrition in July 1969 was at its peak when the Israeli Air Force was performing a series of massive raids on the Egyptian positions at the Canal area. In September 1969 Israel received the state of the art aircraft of the period – F-4 Phantoms with AGM-45 Shrike anti-radar missiles, which was an unprecedented novelty. Israel also sought to purchase tactical ballistic surface-to-surface Lance missiles, but the US did not grant permission to do so, because they could potentially be used as the nuclear warhead carriers.

Egypt's President Nasser, prompted by clear air superiority of Israel over the Suez Canal, once again asked for the assistance of USSR[140]. Only the Soviets were capable to supply a large amount of weapons in a short time. And they agreed. On 18 March 1970 it was revealed that the Soviet assistance would consist of five regiments of the latest MiG-21MF fighters and 150 Soviet volunteer-pilots, selected among the best. In this situation, the US agreed to provide Israel with next 25 F-4 Phantoms and 80 A-4 Skyhawks[141].

Israeli Air Force still was harrassing the objectives in Egypt, but no longer ventured further into the country in order to not provoke the Soviets. There was even

---

[137] The S-125 first saw action on 30 June 1970. It shot down an Israeli F-4 Phantom, and two more were forced to abort their mission. S-125 was a new quality in the Egyptian air defense. See: A. Radomyski, *Gorące niebo...*, p. 74.

[138] A. Radomyski, *Gorące niebo...*, p. 74.

[139] I. Rendall, *Splash one: The story...*

[140] At that time, it was not an easy decision for Egypt, because the politics of this country were slowly shifting their interest toward cooperation with the West, as evidenced by, among others, delivery of French Mirage 5J fighters. Rapid expansion of the Egyptian army by the Soviet Union at the time was slowed down. Even the Soviet crews of the S-125 batteries complained on treatment by their Egyptian allies.

[141] I. Rendall, *Splash one: The story...*

an unwritten agreement: aircraft manned by the Soviet crews would over the area closer than 30 km from the Canal, while Israeli airmen would not attack the Soviets directly[142]. The USSR[143] crews dealt with patrolling the Egyptian air space and Egyptian pilots carried out raids on Israeli forces in the Sinai.

To the east, the Syrian artillery shelled Israeli settlements. In retaliation, the Israeli aircraft bombed targets in Syria. There were several air clashes, in which the Israelis won. Both sides performed the low altitude flights at supersonic speed over the enemy towns and settlements, which was causing damage and chaos.

New missile sites alongside the Canal significantly weakened activity of the Israeli aviation and inflicted many losses, including some of the very valuable F-4 Phantoms. It almost seemed that Egypt supported by the Soviets was gaining initiative[144]. In addition, the Egyptians began to move their batteries closer to the Canal and would soon provide cover for the commando crossings to the other bank. The Egyptian S-75 and S-125 batteries had secured local air superiority in the Canal zone, which reached tens of kilometers deep into the Israeli-occupied Sinai. This had been achieved practically with no participation of Egyptian fighter aircraft and was unique in the history of warfare.

In the meantime, two Egyptian missile boats of the Komar type (type 183R) with a salvo of fours Raduga P-15 Termit (SS-N-2 Styx) surface-to-surface missile the Israeli destroyer INS Eilat (K40)[145]. This was the first time ever when a ship was sunk by a guided missile which had been launched from another vessel. This event echoed around the world and many countries became seriously interested in this kind of weaponry (eg. France then started work on the famous MM-39 Exocet[146], which would inflict heavy losses to Royal Navy in the Falkland Islands in 1982). In retaliation, the formation of eight F-4 Phantoms, performed the longest air-raid mission in the history of Israel, through Sinai, over the Red Sea to Ras Banas, where the Egyptian ship was hit with bombs and sunk. It was a shock for the Egyptians, because it had been thought that this base was beyond the range of the Israeli Air Force.

---

[142] *Ibidem.*

[143] The Soviet pilots flew the aircraft in Egyptian livery. They probably wore Egyptian uniforms.The Israeli fighter ace J. Spektor says, however, that he encountered in the air the MiG-21s with Soviet Red Star markings and these machines differed from the Egyptian aircraft by new shiny lacquer. J. Spektor, *Loud and Clear...*, p. 267

[144] I. Rendall, *Splash one: The story...*

[145] It is sometimes spelt INS Elath. It was a British Z-type destroyer built in 1942–1944. Initially, she served with Royal Navy as HMS Zelaous. A detailed description of sinking of the ship can be found in: K. Kubiak, *Działania sił morskich po drugiej wojnie światowej*, ed. Książka i Wiedza, Warsaw, 2007, pp. 409–412.

[146] K. Kubiak, *Wojna falklandzka 1982*, ed. AJ-Press, Gdańsk, 202, p. 313.

To counteract the dominance of the Egyptian antiaircraft defense, the Israeli Air Force launched a large-scale electronic warfare operation. On 18 July the Israeli F-4s for the first time attacked the Egyptian S-125 site with the latest American electronic warfare pod. The attack was a success, but the Egyptians (the Soviets?) shot down one Phantom. The Israeli Air Force had their hands tied, having been able to attack only the launchers in the immediate vicinity of the Canal and not provoking the Soviets[147]. Nevertheless, they would enter the combat soon. On 25 July a MiG-21MF flown by a Soviet pilot shot down over the Canal an Israeli A-4 with an R-3S (AA-2 Atoll) missile.

This caused some consternation in Israel as it was not known how to react to this fact. Retaliation had been decided. On 30 July four Mirage IIIs headed over the Canal at the altitude of 9,000 m, pretending a reconnaissance mission. They have been identified, and 20 MiG-21MF flown by Soviet pilots took off to intercept thew. In the distance, two flights, each composed of four F-4 Phantom were waiting. Their attack completely surprised the Soviets. Within minutes, they shot down five MiG-21MFs (one with the AIM-9 Sidewinder, one with the medium range AIM-7 Sparrow and with the gunfire). I. Rendall describes this clash[148]: *It has been the biggest air battle since the Six Day War, the outnumbered Israeli pilots, quickly realized weaknesses of the Russians, especially the lack of experience, which immediately came to light: fooled by the Israeli tricks they fired the Atoll missiles (R-3S – JM) blindly.* Previously, he also says: *(...) a MiG exploded, but the pilot managed to eject. Unfortunately, either because of a technical fault or due to pilot error, his parachute opened at once at 9000 m, where there was a penetrating frost, and began to run down slowly to the ground. Some Israeli pilots even used it as a reference point, giving their position in relation to the "frozen Russian".*

The Israeli government did not announce any formal comments on this battle – again – not having intended to provoke the Soviet Union. The Soviets understood, however, that Israeli pilots were extremely difficult opponents who had demonstrated superiority over themselves. Paradoxically, this was met with a certain part of the informal approval by the Egyptians, who had been treated arrogantly by the Soviets. Stories of Egyptian pilots about the exploits of Israeli Phantoms and Mirages proved to be true. This event had a devastating impact on Egypt's forthcoming air combat – the Arab pilots were taking off to fight being aware of the predominance of Israeli fighters in terms of equipment and training. They realized that in cases of meeting an opponent they would most likely be shot down. Morale of the Arab pilots was therefore low.

---

[147] I. Rendall, *Splash one: The story...*
[148] *Ibidem.*

On 7 August 1970 under pressure from the USSR and the USA, the aforementioned ceasefire was signed to end the war of attrition and advanced electronic
warfare duel. As it would turn out, these events had been only a prelude to the next,
much bigger conflict. During the 1,141 days that had passed since the end of the Six
Day War, the Israeli fighters shot down 113 aircraft, another 25 were knocked out
by the Israeli anti aircraft defense (including Hawk missiles). Israel lost two planes
in air clashes and 13 hit by Egyptian anti aircraft batteries (including 5 newest F-4
Phantoms)[149].

During 28 September 1970 Egypt's President Nasser died. He was replaced by
the Gen. Anwar Sadat, who under the guise of relative political stability, was quietly
preparing for the next war and equipping the armed forces with the most modern
weaponry made in USSR. Egyptian air force accounted for 210 modern MiG-
21s, 100 assault subsonic MiG-17s[150], 80 Su-7s and 16 Tupolev Tu-16 bombers[151].
Egypt had also approximately 12 Northrop F-5A fighters and about 14 MiG-17s
sent in by Morocco[152]. In 1973 Egyptian aviation had 650 combat aircraft. The
Egyptians got the latest anti aircraft systems, including 80 2K12 Kub launchers[153]
and more ZSU-23-4s[154]. Concentration of the AA systems alongside the Canal was
so extensive that Egypt gained air cover over a large part of the Israeli-occupied
Sinai. Apparently, in terms of density and depth, the Egyptian air defense system
of the Suez Canal, surpassed even the one around Moscow[155]. Syria received from

---

[149] I. Rendall, *Splash one: The story...*

[150] The Egyptians at Helluan plants near Cairo, modified their MiG-17 aircraft to the assault role and
fiittem them with four underwing racks for 76.2mm unguided missiles cal. 76.2 mm and bomb hardpoints
under the fuselage. In addition to the original Soviet MiG-17s, Egypt was likely to use their Polish copies, the
Lim-5s. See: J. Biziewski, K. Kubiak, *Jom Kippur...*, p. 14; J. Domański, *Samolot myśliwski MiG-17*, ed. MON,
Warsaw, 1976, p. 15 and A. Zbiegniewski, *MiG-i z bazy...*, pp. 42, 48.

[151] All 30Tu-16s held previously by Egypt were destroyed in 1967 as described above. The newly
delivered machines were available in three variants: Tu-16T bomber, recce Tu-16R and Tu-16KSR-2-11
missile carriers (with anti-ship KSR-2 missiles capable also to destroy ground targets). It was an extremely
dangerous weapon.

[152] These F-5A were the only US production fighters at their disposal in the conflict. They were armed
with two 20 mm guns each and AIM-9B Sindewinder missiles. The Moroccans patrolled the Nile Delta
area. Later, in January 1974 at least once they met the Israeli Mirage IIIs and F-4s, no losses reported. See:
M. Gajzler, *Northrop F-5A/B Freedom Fighter*, Pt. I and II, in: "Lotnictwo", Issue No. 3–4/2016.

[153] 2K12 Kub (SA-6 Gainful) set represented new generation of anti-aircraft systems. USSR had
adopted it already in 1965. However, Egypt and Syria received it only several years later. It was armed with
9M9 missiles, 56 kg proximity fuse warhead. Maximum range 17,000 m, 4,000 m minimum, maximum fire
limit 11,000 m,minimum 60 m. The range of a tracking radar 55–70 km (from the surveillance station of
HQ battery). See: J. Biziewski, K. Kubiak, *Jom Kippur...*, p. 38.

[154] In 1973 Egypt had 150 ZSU-23-4 vehicles and Syria 100. They were armed with quadruple AZP-23
23 mm guns. The range of fire is 2,500 m and fire limit 1,600 m. Fire is controlled manually or by a radar,
range 30 km. Accurate fire is possible on the move at speeds up to 25 km/h. This is a very dangerous
weapon, which inflicted on Israeli Air Force a lot of losses. See: J. Biziewski, K. Kubiak, *Jom Kippur...*, p. 39.

[155] I. Rendall, *Splash one: The story...*

the Soviets 200 MiG-21s[156], 120 MiG-17s and 45 Su-7s. In addition a number of Hawker Hunter and MiG-21 aircraft were on lease from Iraq. In total, Syria had 360 combat aircraft (200 MiG-21s, 80 MiG-17s, 80 Su-7s/Su-20s[157]), 100 sets of ZSU-23-4, 60 2K12 Kubs and 36 Mi-4, Mi-6 and Mi-8 helicopters (the same types were owned by the Egyptians). The ratio of the air forces between Israel and its Arab opponents was approximately 1:2 in favour of the Arabs.

Since 1971 Egypt had been receiving very useful gifts from the Soviet Union a very useful – two MiG-25R spy aircraft and two reconnaissance bombers MiG-25RB[158] (NATO code "Foxbat"), together with Soviet crews (6 pilots and technical personnel). They were owned by the USSR but sported Egyptian markings, and their crews wore Egyptian uniforms. They were so secret that the Egyptians had been told that the aircraft were called X-500[159]. They performed spy flights over the Sinai and Israel at a ceiling of 21,000–22,000 m at a speed of about 3 Ma[160]. The Israeli F-4 Phantoms repeatedly tried to shoot them down with the medium-range AIM-7 Sparrow missiles, firing at a sharp angle upward from 14,000 m, but the MiG-25 was too fast and flew too high. Attempts were also made to reach them with the ground-based MIM-23 Hawk missiles. However, they failed to down any "Egyptian" Foxbat.

Transfer of these four MiG-25Rs/RBs, together with the personnel and technical equipment from the Soviet Union to Egypt, required as many as 60 transport aircraft (4 heavy An-22s and 56 medium An-12s). The first test flight of the MiG-25 in the Egyptian livery took place on 26 March 1971. On average, it was planned to perform two spy flights of spy per month, always to be carried out by a pair of the aircraft. Timetable of takeoffs and landings could not be fixed, flights were to be held in complete radio silence. Takeoffs and landings were to be covered by the Soviet manned MiG-21SMs.

---

[156] Despite the supplies from the Soviet Union and Poland, Syria also bought 15 MiG-21F13s in Hungary and 12 in Czechoslovakia (Aero S-106) as well as 12 MiG-21Ms in the GDR.

[157] M. Musella, *Air Operations During The 1973 Arab-Israeli War And The Implications For Marine Aviation*, Marine Corps Command and Staff College in 1985, the material available on the website: www.globalsecurity.org/military/library/report/1985/MML.htm

[158] M. Mikołajczuk, J. Gruszczyński, *MiG-25RB niezwykły czterdziestolatek*, Pt. 2, in: "Lotnictwo", Issue No. 7/2010. Data on this unusual machine can also be found in: J. Gordon, O, Putmakow, *MiG-25...*, pp. 28–41 and D. Richardson, *Współczesne samoloty rozpoznawcze*, ed. BGW, Warsaw, 1992, pp. 34–35.

[159] P. Butowski, *MiG-25...*, p. 10.

[160] Officially, the flight manual for the MiG-25R allowed for impassable speed of 2.85 Ma (3000 km/h), though sometimes they were flown faster. Israeli radars once established the presence of the MiG-25 speeding 3.2 Ma, which was fleeing the Israeli fighters and missiles. MiG-25 could maintain such a speed for a short period of time. Initially, a maximum speed of only 3 minutes, but for the needs of the conflict over Israel the time was extended to 8 minutes. The engine thrust allowed to achieve higher speeds, however, but it must have been limited due to overheating of the structure (at high speeds pilots complained about unbearable heat in the cockpit). See: Ibid, p. 10.

The first operational flight took place on 10 October 1971. A pair of MiG-25s flew over the Mediterranean Sea at an altitude of 22,000 m reached the vicinity of Haifa, Tel Aviv, and then returned to the base at Port Said in Egypt. On 6 November 1971 a pair of MiG-25s took off from the Cairo-West air base and was reconnoitring the Sinai. The Israeli F-4 Phantoms and the Mirage IIICJs failed to intercept the intruders. The Soviets quickly figured out that the Israeli air defense is put on full alert along the flight route of MiG-25s. This meant that Israel had to receive information about takeoff of each Foxbat. Then the Soviets stopped to notify the Egyptians about their flight plans and takeoffs were carried out at random times (ie. after an engine test). The Soviets recall that every time after such an unexpected takeoff, many Egyptians suddenly ran somewhere to make a phone call[161]. Most likely, many of them had been bribed by Israeli intelligence, which indicates the low morale of the Egyptian personnel.

On 7 November Israeli Defense Minister Moshe Dayan admitted that in view of these flights, the Israeli armed forces were powerless. It was recognized that if the Soviets decided to conduct bomb attacks with MiG-25RBs, Israel would not be able to stop them. The only thing that had been left were protests notes to the United Nations.

In the 1971–1973 the MiG-25s performed many more combat reconnaissance flights over Sinai and Israel, providing invaluable information to the Egyptians. The last MiG-25 was withdrawn from Egypt to the Soviet Union in May 1975. Some sources indicate that in the early 70's the Soviets sent to Egypt also their Su-15 (Flagon) fighters together with crews, but this has not been yet confirmed[162].

The air force had also been constantly modernized by Israel. In 1973 a modernized version of Nesher called IAI Kfir was developed[163]. It was a multirole fighter aircraft equipped with the General Electric J79 engine of the F-4 Phantom. The air-to-air Shafrir missile, designed in 1961 and modelled on the American AIM-9 Sindewinder had been upgraded as well. Opinions about it varied. Some references claim it was successful and accurate[164], but in practice many Shafrirs missed their targets. In 1973 Israel already had 120 F-4 Phantoms (including 6 very expensive reconnaissance RF-4Es), 160 A-4 Skyhawks, 70 Mirage IIICJs/IAI Neshers/IAI Kfirs and 16 obsolete Super Mystere, as well as a number of even older Vatours. Israel also built at that time its first unmanned reconnaissance aircraft.

Meanwhile, many skirmishes took place having indicated how fragile peace in the Middle East was. For example, on 13 September 1973 a squadron of Mirage IIICJs

---

[161] P. Butowski, *MiG-25...*, p. 10.

[162] P. Butowski, V. Pankov, V. Ponomariev, *Su-15 Flagon*, ed. AJ-Press, Gdańsk, 1994, p. 15 and A. Glass, *Samoloty '85*, ed. NOT-Sigma, Warsaw, 1986, p. 40.

[163] R. Kwas, M. Gołembiewski, *IAI Kfir*, ed. AJ-Press, Gdynia, 1996, p. 3.

[164] I. Rendall, *Splash one: The story...*

and F-4 Phantoms was patrolling the coast of Syria and came upon the formation of several dozen MiG-21. In the air combat, where 13 MiGs were shot down for a loss of one Mirage.

On 5 October Israeli intelligence reported that the armies of Egypt and Syria had deployed close to the Israel borders. Israel had a plan for pre-emptive strike (similar to the operation "MOKED" of 1967). However, Prime Minister Golda Meir did not consent to this attack, as she was afraid Israel would be considered a formal aggressor[165].

Fighting in October 1973

On Saturday 6 October 1973 there was the Jewish holiday of Yom Kippur (Day of Atonement). The streets of Israeli cities and towns were deserted. The Arabs decided to use it as a factor of surprise. About 14.00 hrs the Egyptians and Syrians attacked the Israeli at the Suez Canal and Golan Heights[166]. The surprised Israeli troops buckled under the assault. The Egyptians broke through fortifications at the Suez Canal, and then the force of 70,000 men supported by tanks breached several kilometers deep into the Sinai. The Egyptian army was actively supported by the air force. The fighter-bombers (mainly the very efficient Su-7BMKs), performed about 200 sorties against Israeli troops in the Sinai, having destroyed about 400 military facilities. Israeli air base Rephidim in the central part of the peninsula was almost eliminated by a couple of raids of the Egyptian Su-7s. According to the Egyptians, at that time the effectiveness of their raids reached 95%. The Tu-16KSR bombers flying over the Mediterranean stroke the Israeli command posts, radar sites and air bases with winged long-range KSR-2 (AS-5 Kelt) missiles. Inn this way, at least three Israeli radar stations had been destroyed. Israeli anti aircraft defense probably managed to shoot down one Tu-16[167]. In the area of the Golan Heights, the Syrian air force performed similar raids on Israeli positions, having inflicced heavy casualties for a loss of only one aircraft. The heli-lifted Syrian commandos neutralized the Israeli radio-electronic listening station on Mount Hermon. Then five Syrian divisions, 70,000 men strong and with more than 1,000 tanks[168] commenced the attack. The local Israeli force was only 8,000 men strong and had to withdraw.

Israel had been surprised and the Arabs became more and more confident. Theoretically it was now possible to re-capture the territories lost in 1967 – the Golan Heights and the Sinai Peninsula – but even to pose a threat to the existence of the State of Israel. For such an occasion the Arab world had been waiting for decades.

---

[165] *Ibidem.*
[166] *Ibidem.*
[167] J. Biziewski, K. Kubiak, *Jom Kippur...*, p. 46.
[168] I. Rendall, *Splash one: The story...*

The Israeli Air Force was unable to concentrate their effort, because the opponents were strongly attacking from both the west (Sinai), and from the east (the Golan Heights). The Arabs had been aware of the weaknesses of their own fighter aircraft when compared to Israelis, so the task of air cover for their own troops was entrusted mainly to the land-based air defense. The Egyptian and Syrian anti-aircraft defense consisted of S-75, S-125, 2K12 Kub, ZSU-23-4 systems and the Striela MANPADS. Indeed, the ground-based systems (especially the S-125s and Kubs, then proof to electronic warfare systems) inflicted many losses on Israeli Air Force. According to the plans of Arab high command, the Egyptian and Syrian troops were to halt the advance from to time, dig in and await the Israeli Air Force attacks, repulse them with anti-aircraft defense systems. After having inflicted substantial losses on the enemy aviation, the Arab formations were to continue the advance.

The Israeli jet fighters were the most effective against the Arab MiGs. But in combat against the ground systems they suffered heavy losses and the effects of their actions were often meager. Of necessity, however, they were performing such missions. In the first 30 minutes of the raid on the Egyptian troops, Israel lost five A-4 Skyhawk and another five F-4 Phantoms. During the first hours of war, the Arabs fired about 1,500 ground-to-air missiles, but only 1.5% of them were accurate[169]. It was enough, however, to inflict severe losses on Israeli aviation. More Israeli machines were downed by the ZSU-23-4 gun systems.

On the Golan Heights, the Israeli Air Force lost another 25 A-4s and 5 F-4s. A total of 40 Israeli aircraft had already been downed – 10% of the combat strength of the country's air forces. Another 60 Israeli machines were heavily damaged, many experienced pilots were killed. Israel could not afford such high losses, so pilots had been forbidden to venture further than 15 km beyond the Canal

The situation in the east was even worse. There, the Syrian tanks crossed the buffer line established in 1967. The Israeli Phantoms and Skyhawks were thrown into battle as direct support aircraft while Mirage IIIs and IAI Neshers were engaging Syrian aircraft. On the second day the Syrians overwhelmed the Israeli armour on the Golan Heights and were advancing further.

The greatest threat to the Israeli Air Force were 2K12 Kub systems (which could change the frequency of the radar and were therefore resistant to the Israeli systems of electronic disruption). Israeli Air Force managed to hit the control computer of integrated network of air defense of Syria, having silenced the air defense over a large area. Immediately the Phantoms and Skyhawks took off and destroyed many Syrian vehicles. Part of the Israeli aviation's attacks were carried out from the air space over Lebanon[170].

---

[169] *Ibidem*, p. 175.
[170] J. Biziewski, K. Kubiak, *Jom Kippur...*, p. 45.

The next day, the Egyptian air force continued to harass positions of the Israeli troops, while the Israeli Air Force decided to breach the air defence on the Suez Canal and to eliminated seven Egyptian airfields. This time, however, it was a difficult task. The Egyptians hid their aircraft in shelters and had special runway repair personnel. Neverteless the Israelis managed to inflict heavy losses on the Egyptian air bases. They also attacked the Egyptian bridges on the Canal. Fairly heavy losses were suffered (including loss of five Phantoms). The use of the same tactics that had been applied to break the Syrian air defense was not possible against Egypt, as this would mean heavy losses. It was necessary to come up with another way to destroy the S-125 and 2K12 Kub systems. Since their destruction from the air in a given situation was had been considered hazardous, they had to be destroyed by the land troops. It was an unprecedented and bizarre situation, when the Israeli army got the task of destroying the anti-aircraft systems to make possible operations of their own aviation[171]. The Israeli troops managed to open the corridor in the Egyptian positions, through which their aircraft was capable to operate.

Fighting on the Golan Heights was still fierce. Israel made a good use of the unmanned aerial vehicles, both for recconnaissance or as mock targets, as well as the emission of statics[172]. The Syrian radar crews did not distinguish them from aircraft and switched to the active mode, thus facilitating guidance of the AGM-45A Shrike anti-radar missile. Among the unmanned aerial vehicles were the American MQM-74 Telem, Teledyne Ryan AQM-34H/Model 124I Mabat (dropped by the C-130 transport aircraft), which could stay in the air for 75 minutes, and Northrop MQM-74 as well as Teledyne Ryan 174 .

At the end of the second day of the war the Syrian anti-aircraft defense had already been heavily strained, and was no longer able to protect armoured troops that would decimated by the Israeli Air oFrce. After the tanks had been destroyed, the Israeli jest fighters ventured into Syria, where anti-aircraft system was admittedly still intact, but much less numerous. In three days, the Israeli Air Force annihilated the Syrian air defense. They destroyed not only the ground-based launchers, but in aerial combat they shot down 32 Syrian fighters.

During the first three days of the war, Israel had lost more than 50 aircraft, but thanks to the efforts of the air force, the situation was getting stabilized. All parties of the conflict have been exhausted, and asked their allies for support. The Arabs requested the Soviet Union for more anti aircraft systems and missiles, Israel intervened with the US for further F-4, A-4, AGM-45 Shrike missiles and the last electronic warfare systems.

---

[171] *Ibidem* p. 147.
[172] S. J. Zaloga, *Unmanned aerial vechicles*, ed. Osprey, 2008, pp. 21, 27.

At that time, the Israeli army has already advanced deep into Syrian territorym having captured a lot of fuel dumps. Then the Syrians withdrew the majority of anti aircraft systems from the frontline to the rear, where they were to protect the strategic centres of the state. Air cover of the troops on the frontline was entrusted to the MiGs, which would however quickly fall victim to the Israeli fighters. The air combat ratio of losses in the area was 25:1 in favour of Israel. During the first four days War, Syria lost about 50% of the fighter aircraft and anti-aircraft systems, and the Israeli Air Force on this front lost only 6 machines. Israel regained domination in the air. Both flying and ground did their best. For example, of 236 Israeli planes that had returned to base damaged, 215 were repaired and fully operational. The Syrians had launched several ballistic R-7 (SS-1 Scud) missiles at civilian targets in the Galilee, which was met with retaliatory Israeli air raid on the building of the Ministry of Defence in Damascus[173].

At that time, Iraq attempted to give some support to its Arab allies. The armoured brigade, moving from Baghdad to Damascus was detected, however, by the Israeli aircraft. First, Israeli commandos blew up the bridge and mined the road, and eventually the virtually immobilized Iraqi armoured unit was destroyed from the air by Israeli Phantoms.

On 11 October at the airport in Damascus began to land Soviet transport aircraft with the new supplies. On 14 October the Israeli Air Force penetrated the air defence barrier around the Syrian capital and dropped bombs on the airport, having destroyed new equipment still in crates and possibly hit some Soviet transports (An-12?).

On the same day the Egyptian army attempted to commence another armoured offensive and advanced toward Gidi and Mitla passes. The Egyptian air force raided Israeli positions, but the Israeli tanks backed by aircraft had managed to survive the attack and took over the initiative. Then the largest tank battle since the World War II had occured[174]. Within several hours Egypt suffered more than 1,000 casualties, lost about 260 tanks and 200 other armoured vehicles. The Israeli army lost about 40 tanks[175]. In addition, Israeli fighter planes shot down 10 enemy aircraft with no losses of their own.

After the Egyptian air defenses alongside the Canal had been incapacitated (as descibed above), the Egyptians copied the Syrians' mistake by having sent into the air a number of fighters to provide air cover for their ground troops. Just as over Syria, the Arab MiGs were also decimated. On the western front gained air supremacy as well.

Having controlled both fronts, the Israeli Air Force could now threaten Cairo itself. On 22 October the Israeli armoured brigade retook Mount Hermon in the Golan

---

[173] J. Biziewski, K. Kubiak, *Jom Kippur...*, p. 45.
[174] I. Rendall, *Splash one: The story...*
[175] J. Biziewski, K. Kubiak, *Jom Kippur...*, p. 24.

Heights, which overlooked the nearby area. On the western front, the Egyptian 3rd Army was encircled. Israel could decimate it from the air, or force them to surrender.

At the time, US satellites detected south of Cairo the R-7 (SS-1 Scud) ballistic missile sites[176]. It was a very important discovery, because in the event especially they would have been used (especially armed with mass destruction warheads), Israel could theoretically respond with the nuclear weapons, too[177]. In the face of danger, the UN called on both sides to stop the fighting. On 22 October it proposed a demarkation line to Israel, Syria and Egypt dividing. Egypt and Syria – now defeated – were willing to accept it, but Israel, which had restored self-confidence, did not intend to withdraw from western bank of the Canal. To verify that the ceasefire was respected, on 22 October the Soviets sent their Egypt-stationed MiG-25RB to recconnoitre the front line. The photographs showed that fighting in some areas are continued[178]. Then the US and USSR diplomacies entered the scene. Eventually, on 25 October the conflict ended. Then, the Soviets performed three more recce flights of their MiG-25s, which proved that the fighting had actually ceased.

However, a political conflict began. Sadat demanded that the United States and the Soviet Union should bring in their peacemaking troops. The USSR actually began to ferry their transport aircraft with equipment and troops to air bases in Yugoslavia, from where within few hours they would be ready to take off to Syria and Egypt[179]. RAF reported that about 70 Soviet vessels had been detected in the Mediterranean Sea. The American air lift was launched on 12 October, when the USAF transport aircraft landed in El Arish. Over the next two days, the Americans would perform 566 flights to Israel (421 C-141 and 145 C-5 Galaxy), having supplied 22,300 tons of equipment[180]. Israel received, among others, more AGM-45 Shrike anti-radar missiles, the AGM-65

---

[176] The Egyptians asked the Soviet Union to sell nuclear weapons to them in order to counterbalance Israel' possibilities. The Soviets refused and gave them a nuclear guarantee instead. At that time, the American satellite noticed a cargo having been unloaded from Soviet vessels at Alexandria, which was identified as the likely nuclear bombs. Then they were taken to the Egyptian air force base inland. It was an important warning and forced the Great Powers to act for peace in the region. See I. Rendall, *Splash one: The story*....

[177] Israel had been interested in nuclear weapons from the 1940's. In the late 50's, in return for help of the Israeli armed forces during the battles of the Suez Canal, the French built a small reactor in Israel for civilian purposes. However this was the basis for further work on nuclear weapons. In 1973 the Israeli air force ahad probably 13 ready to use nuclear bombs and ballistic missiles with nuclear Jericho warheads. Some sources suggest that Israel contemplated their use against Egypt and put them in a state of combat readiness on the night of 6/7 October 1973. These bombs, carried by the Phantoms and Kfirs were to be used against Egyptian troops if they would have managed to penetrate deep into the Sinai. Besides, even one such bomb dropped in the Nile delta could eliminate the Egyptian economy, highly dependent on agriculture on the banks of the river. This information was apparently obtained from intelligence sources and handed over to President Nixon, who ordered the immediate delivery of a large number of modern conventional weapons to Israel. See J. Biziewski, K. Kubiak, *Jom Kippur...*, p. 28, I. Rendall, *Splash one: The story...*

[178] M. Mikołajczuk, J. Gruszczyński, *MiG-25RB...*, p. 61.

[179] I. Rendall, *Splash one: The story...*

[180] J. Biziewski, K. Kubiak, *Jom Kippur...*, p. 48.

Maverick air-to-surface missiles, next AIM-9 Sindewinders and the Rockey guided bombs. Israel Air Force also received 12 C-130 transports, 30 helicopters, 6 antiaircraft batteries and a new electronic warfare pods. President Nixon put the US forces wordlwide in a state of high alert. The situation was very tense and therefore fearful parties of the conflict finally signed a full ceasefire on 27 October.

Israel defeated Egypt and Syria mainly due to flexible reaction of the IAF. Aviation proved to be a decisive factor, able to effectively support the land forces fighting on two fronts, against more numerous opponents. This was largely the battle of doctrines: flexible Israeli defence and Arab doctrine based on the principles of the Soviet Army and the Warsaw Pact. A relatively small number of Israeli fighter jets managed to drive a wedge in the closed system of the opponent's defence and supported the ground troops in making the breakthrough. This caused a collapse of the air-defence system based on Soviet principles, inflexible and relying on the absolute supremacy of ground-based command posts. Without a central command system, Arab fighters were no match for the Israeli pilots and suffered heavy losses[181]. Israel claims that its fighters destroyed 334 aircraft in air combat, of which 60 by gunfire, and the remainder with Shafrir and AIM-9B missiles. Another 180 Arab planes were shot down by the Hawk systems and anti-aircraft guns. The Arabs admit they had lost 440 aircraft. Israel lost 103–110 combat aircraft (depending on the source), which accounted for 20% of the pre-war strength (including more than half of the A-4 Skyhawks). For majority of the losses inflicted on the Israeli Air Force the ground-based systems were responsible (40 by the S-75s, 10 by 2K12 Kubs, 4 by Striela MANPADS and 40 by the ZSU-23-4 vehicles). Israel believes that in the air battles it had lost only three aircraft. The Arabs claim that their MiGs shot down at least 20 enemy machines[182]. Quite effective proved to be the DEFA 5–52 30 mm of Mirage III and M-61 Vulcan F-4 Phantom cannons. Seldom and with no success the medium-range Matra R.530 (Mirage III) and Sparrow AIM-7 (F-4 Phantom) were fired. The Soviet R-3S missiles (NATO code: AA-2 Atoll, a copy of the American AIM-9B Sindewinder) proved to be less effective than their American counterparts[183]. While in 1967 95% of aircraft lost by the Arabs were the machines destroyed on the ground in 1973 the Egyptian losses in air bases amounted to only 6% and 10% in case of Syria.

---

[181] Reverse situations, when Arab fighters took over the initiative, were sporadic, although sometimes they occurred. For example, on 14 October a large group of Israeli aircraft (including 70 F-4 Phantoms), carried out air strikes on the Egyptian positions in the Nile valley. Israeli formation was intercepted by the Egyptian MiG-21 fighters, which with in 50 minutes shot down to 18 F-4 Phantoms for a loss of only 4 machines. Although these are Egyptian figures Israel has never denied. See J. Biziewski, K. Kubiak, *Jom Kippur...*, p. 48.

[182] J. Biziewski, K. Kubiak, *Jom Kippur...*, p. 48.

[183] *Ibidem*, p. 46.

As many as 84% of the losses of the Egyptian aviation and 80% of the Syrian air force were sufferered the air (the remainder were probably the aircraft lost due to technical reasons). Israel lost in the air just a small percentage of about a total of 110 aircraft destroyed[184].

It is also worth mentioning that among the aircraft lost by the Arab states as many as 61 were downed by a friendly fire (44 by Kubsand 15 by the S-75s and S-125s)[185].

An important role was played by the reconnaissance aircraft. Israel used for this purpose both costly and specialized RF-4E Phantoms and Mirage IIIs, as well as the ordinary combat aircraft. The radar reconnaissance was conducted by Vatour ground attack aircraft and Noratlas transports specially adapted for the purpose.

The Arab countries' air forces probably do not have specialized reconnaissance aircraft (not including the Soviet MiG-25R in Egypt) and underestimated aerial reconnaissance. The Arabs also feared that a single reconnaissance plane can be shot down by own troops, which had happened quite often[186].

The doctrine applied in this conflict was much like the one of the Six Day War. Israel was not a member of NATO, hence it had formulated its own views on the use of aviation, which were modifications of the operations and decisive blow of 1967. The American experiences of the Vietnam War had also been taken into account. In turn, the Arab states applied almost perfect copy of the Warsaw Pact. Israel was to be crushed by masses of land troops, supported by masses of aircraft inferior to the enemy in terms of technology and armament[187]. Once again, the world powers, afraid of further escalation, suspended the arms supplies to their Middle East allies.

2.4. Operation "Peace for Galilee", the Bekaa Valley (Lebanon) 1982

After the Arab armies had been defeated by Israel in 1973 Egyptian President Sadat realized that victory over the Israeli armed forces was virtually impossible. He concluded that the only way to have any impact on Israel was maintaining relations with the United States. The US was the only country that could influence Israel. Sadat decided to get politically closer to the West, while freezing relations with the USSR at the same time. In 1977 Sadat gave an unprecedented speech in the Israeli parliament (Knesset), which would result in a peace treaty between Egypt

---

[184] *Ibidem*, p. 48.

[185] *Ibidem*. Functional scheme of the Egyptian antiaircraft system during the Yom Kippur War is in: A. Swanson, M. Swanson, *Military Atlas...*

[186] *Ibidem*, p. 47.

[187] It is worth noting that during the Yom Kippur War the greatest tank combat since World War II took place. On all fronts about 2000 tanks of all parties were fighting, of which Egypt lost 264. The Soviet concept of mass armed forces also on the ground had proven to be inferior than Western-Israeli concept of smaller, mobile forces, well-trained and with modern equipment. More about the conflict is in: A. Swanson, M. Swanson, *Military Atlas...* and D. Hill (ed.), *Kronika wojen...*, p. 230.

and Israel signed on 18 September 1978. Egypt recognized the state of Israel, and the Sinai returned to Egypt[188].

In 1978 US Congress agreed to sell modern weaponry to Egypt and Saudi Arabia (which also maintained good relations with the West), which just a few years earlier would have been absolutely impossible. Soon to Egypt received 35 F-4 Phantoms and the 40 state-of-the-art F-16As. Saudi Arabia purchased modern F-15 fighter jets and AWACS early-warning aircraft, the converted Boeing 707 aircraft. Egypt in turn provided with some Soviet equipment to the United States, where it would be tested. For example, the Americans obtained at least one MiG-23, which participated in the test flights with the USAF as an YF-113 and was stationed at the Nellis base in Nevada.

In order to maintain balance, to Israel 75 F-16As were delivered, and after long negotiations, the US agreed to provide the 25 F-15s ($ 24 million apiece). Two years later, Israel received 26 latest F-15Cs and two early-warning E-2C Hawkeye aircraft[189].

Egypt's recognition of the state of Israel and the peace treaty provoked angry reactions in the Arab world. Syria and Iraq had not followed the pro-Western course and remained under the influence of the Soviet Union (although Iraq also collaborated with the West and bought Western equipment for the needs of the war with Iran). Syria also established renewed contacts with the Palestine Liberation Organization (PLO), which carried out numerous actions against Israel. PLO with the support of the Syrian army had set up a secret base in formally neutral Lebanon, from where it made terrorist attacks on Israeli settlements. The most notorious of the terrorist actions of this period was the PLO's attack on a hotel in the heart of Tel Aviv itself.

In retaliation for terrorist attacks, the Israeli Air Force bombed PLO bases in Lebanon. For Lebanon had disastrous consequences. So far it had been a state with a quite stable economy and relatively high prosperity. Society was divided into mainly Muslim and Christian communities, which lived side by side without major conflicts with each other. Unfortunately, the entry of Israeli troops changed the situation completely. In 1975 a civil warbroke out between Muslims supported by the PLO and Syria, and Christians supported by Israel. The war has divided the nation and has devastated the state. Lebanon has never regained its former glory.

The Israeli Air Force, supported by unmanned aircraft, was performing numerous raids on positions of the PLO and Muslim Lebanese militants. After some time, the United Nations negotiated a ceasefire, having given Israel right to occupy a large part of southern Lebanon. For a while, the PLO terrorist attacks ceased, however, then again they increased, this time from the bases located more to the north. Israel reacted with more air raids.

---

[188] I. Rendall, *Splash one: The story...*
[189] *Ibidem*, p. 206.

Israel had an informal arrangement with Syria, it would not attack the regular Syrian Army. Israel was free to fight the PLO as long as it would not make any hostile steps towards the Syrians.

Syria was aware that the system was a short-lived and just in case, commenced to build an air defence system in the Bekaa Valley, northeast of Beirut.

At the beginning of June first clashes had occurred in the air and in about a month they developed into the full-scale air war. A. Poray says that on 7 June two Syrian MiG-23MFs two Israeli F-16As with R-23 (AA-7 Apex) missiles. One of the MiGs was downed a moment later by the F-15A with the Python-31 missile[190]. The next day, the Israeli MD-500 helicopters destroyed without any major problems, two P-15 radar sites. The Syrians had not drawn any conclusions from that. On the same day there were still air skirmishes with losses on both sides, where the MiG-23MS aircraft shot down at least one F-16A[191]. Several MiG-21s and MiG-23s were downed by the F-15s. On 9 June there was a between the groups MiG-23MFs and F-16As, when both sides lost one fighter each[192].

The aforementioned Israeli-Syrian agreement was finally broken when on 27 June 1979 the Israeli F-4 Phantoms and A-4 Skyhawks raided the Syrian positions near Sidon in southern Lebanon[193]. From a ceiling of 6,000 m they were covered by the F-15s and IAI Kfir's. The action had been controlled by the E-2C Hawkeye, which detected two approaching squadrons of Syrian MiG-21s. Immediately the fighter cover was guided at them. After a few minutes of the ensuing combat the F-15s and Kfirs shot down a total of five MiGs, without any losses. F-15 won the first victory in its history. The latest missiles AIM-9L Sindewinder proved very effective. In contrast to the earlier variants (eg. The AIM-9B, or their Soviet copies, the R-3S missiles as used by the Syrians) could hit the target when fired even from the front hemisphere. Not a single MiG did not make it through cover and was not able to threaten the F-4s and A-4s attacking ground targets. It was a demonstration of the latest military technology, i.e. control over the aircraft by an early warning airborne radar from a very long range.

The most modern fighter jets of the Israeli Air Force once again took part in combat three months later, when on 19 September a flight of four F-15 was covering a single RF-4E Phantom during a reconnaissance mission over Lebanon. This group

---

[190] A. Poray, *Pierwsza wojna libańska*, Part 2, "Skrzydlata Polska", Issue No. 3/2010. This report is all the more surprising that officially no F-16 has ever been shot down by enemy aircraft. The fact that this information was published by the "Skrzydlata Polska", indicates that it was very probable. The F-16A armed only with short-range AIM-9s actually could be relatively easily downed by MiG-23MF with medium-range R-23s, if the nearby F-15s (armed with the medium-range AIM-7s) had not managed to react in time, which could have been the case in the event described herein).

[191] A. Poray, *Pierwsza...*, p. 52.

[192] *Ibidem.*

[193] I. Rendall, *Splash one: The story...*

was attacked by a squadron of the Syrian MiG-23MFs[194], which fired several R-60 missiles. But they all missed. The Israeli fighter jets immediately took advantage of this moment and tried to attack. Then the MiGs at full thrust withdrew from the fight, and the F-15 could not leave the reconnaissance Phantom alone. After a moment, another Syrian formation attacked, this time it was composed of the MiG-21MFs (NATO code: "Fishbed J"[195]). Within minutes the F-15s downed two of them, one with the Shafrir missile, the second by a gunfire. The recce mission had been completed, so the F-15s once again fulfilled their role and without any losses.

It is worth mentioning that in these clashes the medium range air-to-air missiles had not been used (F-15 could carry theAIM-7 Sparrow, MiG-23MF the R-23 missiles). Only short range missiles like AIM-9L, Shafrir, R-3S and R-60 were fired. This was probably due to the fact that those days the medium-range missiles were still underdeveloped and innaccurate. In Vietnam, usually for a few or a dozen AIM-7s fired, only one or two directly hit the target. Shooting down the plane with a single medium-range missile was very rare then. The missiles were used rather to "hit the cauldron," or to break up the formation of enemy planes at the start of air combat. The missiles having exploded between them caused fear among pilots, who were fleeing in different directions.

In 1981 fighting in Lebanon continued with the active participation of Israeli aircraft, which still retained their air supremacy[196]. The Syrians, from time to time tried to counter this by acquisition of the most modern weaponry in the USSR. On 13 February 1981 the Israeli reconnaissance aircraft RF-4E once again performed the task over Lebanon, escorted by the F-15s. Israeli formation was flying at high altitude. At one point it encountered a pair of the MiG-25P heavy interceptors (NATO code: "Foxbat"), recently imported from the Soviet Union, as the countermeasure against the F-15s[197]. Israeli pilots, however, kept a cool head and made use of their asset of electronic advantage over the mighty Soviet "Foxbat". They

---

[194] Given that these MiGs fired one of the newest then Soviet R-60 missiles, it can be assumed that these were the MiG-23MFs (which could carry these missiles). Older version of the MiG-23MS, had equipment and weapons taken from the MiG-21MF, that is, the RS-2U, R-3S and R-3R missiles. The MiG-23MF with R-23, R-60 and K-13M missiles theory were capable to shoot down any Israeli plane (including F-16A) had they not been covered by the F-15s and an early warning E 2C Hawkeye aircraft.

[195] Western sometimes claim these were the MiG-21J, but such a variant never existed. Undoubtedly these were the MiG-21MFs, which in the NATO code were called Fishbed J.

[196] R. Ball, *Camuflage & markings – the Israeli Air Force*, Part Two: 1967 to 2001, ed. Guideline Publications, UK, 2001, pp. 68–72.

[197] MiG-25P was armed with heavy air-to-air R-40 missiles (NATO code: AA-6 Acrid) with a range of about 40 km, so in theory it was capable to threaten the F-15, though inferior to its US counterpart in terms of electronics. Undoubtedly, the MiG-25P was able to shoot down any aircraft owned by Israel, including the Kfir and F-16A, which had no air-to-air medium-range missiles necessary to combat this plane. MiG-25 could speed at 3 Ma and no other fighter could match it. See P. Butowski, *MiG-25, MiG-31*, ed. AJ-Press, Gdańsk, 1991, p. 12.

switched on their modern systems of electronic warfare (ie. ECM) and they turned back not to come within range of enemy missiles. In the meantime, the F-15s fired large quantities of film strips, to impede their detection. The MiGs blinded ECM systems, several times tried to renew the attack, but they could not determine the position of the Israeli formation. At that time, the E-2C guided the F-15s to a good position to attack. After a while, they fired a volley of missiles AIM-7 Sparrow, hitting one "Foxbat"[198]. The other managed to escape. It was the first downing of an MiG-25 in the history.

A period of relative calm in the air from that moment on was interfered by individual clashes. For example, on 21 April the Israeli fighter jets shot down two MiG-23s, and on 26 May two more MiG-21s was downed by the F-16As. In the meantime, the Syrians deployed in the Bekaa Valley the 2K12 Kub systems (SA-6 Gainful). Under their protection on 28 April the Syrian Mi-8 helicopters tried to lift some PLO guerillas to the north of Lebanon, but two of them were shot down by the F-16As.

Over the Bekaa Valley constantly operated the unmanned aerial vehicles – the Scouts and Mastiffs – which were carrying out the electronic recce missions. Crews of the Syrian 2K12 Kubs and other stations[199] activated their radars in such cases and inadvertently revealed information on frequency and radar mode of work. This information proved invaluable later when the ECM systems used by the Israeli Air Force would be programmed. If the Syrians had decided not to turn on their radar, they were blind and unveil the vast areas to the Israeli Air Force. The operators of unmanned aerial vehicles took advantage of this and their machines took off for the undisturbed observation and surveillance missions.

---

[198] I. Rendall, *Splash one: The story...*

[199] A. Poray says: The Syrian troops in the Bekaa Valley gathered relatively numerous air defence units. According to the assumptions of the high command, these forces were to be a major counterbalance to Israeli aviation. In the Syrian armed forces, the air defense troops enjoyed considerable respect and were extremely numerous. With them served up to 20–25% of the total number of Syrian soldiers. Despite this, both the level of technology and the level of training were far from satisfactory. The system of radar stations was relatively well developed. Theere were more than 100 radars – P-12, P-14, P-15, P-35, P-37. They were mostly older types, prone to interferences. The P-35, P-37 and a radio altimeter PRW-11 could function only in areas free from interference. The P-12 and P-18 were resistant to interference only in a narrow range. Just a few – P-14F, P-19 and P-40 had higher performance, except that P-19 and P-40 had been located near Damascus, in the Bekaa Valley the most modern stations were the P-14Fs. The P-15s were resistant to low and medium interference but locating their sites in the mountains effectively abrogated their pros. The mountain slopes reflected their waves which caused natural jamming. Overall, the Syrian air defence system was able to work at interferences 5–10 Wt/MHz or 30–40 Wt/MHz at certain spots. In the border region, this system was capable to track to 150–200 airborne targets. This system however was automated, the units had virtually no autonomy of action and were dependent on the central command. It was a cause of significant delays (about 6–8 minutes) in transmission of commands and information. It was a time sufficient for the Israeli aircraft to reach the targets in southern Lebanon. These deficiencies also caused a lot of errors in determining the bearings of targets. Source: A. Poray, *Pierwsza wojna libańska*, Part One, in: "Skrzydlata Polska", Issue No. 2/2010.

The Syrians sent in response to the Bekaa Valley more 2K12 Kub systems, which met with protest of the Israelis. They threatened had the Syrians not withdrawn them, the systems would be attacked. At that time, however, Israel did not carry out any raids on these facilities, probably because it feared the presence of the Soviet crews. Possible casualities could cause political conflict with the Soviet Union.

In June and July 1981 Lebanon fighting with the PLO guerillas continued. Their artillery was bombarding Israeli settlements across the border (later evacuated). On 17 July the Israeli aircraft bombed the PLO headquarters in Beirut and killed several hundred people. As a result, the US the scene and forced a temporary truce. Israel, however, retained the right to carry out reconnaissance flights over Lebanon. On 29 July an Israeli RF-4E Phantom, escorted by the F-15s, was again attacked by the MiG-25Ps. Once again, the escort managed to shoot down one "Foxbat".

The truce was finally broken in the spring of 1982. The PLO intensified shelling and Israel renewed bombing. This time the Israeli supreme command decided to commence the ultimate attempt to defeat the enemy. A plan for the operation "Peace for Galilee" called for an overwhelming invasion of southern Lebanon in order to displace the PLO from there once and for all. This required neutralization of the Syrian air defence system in the Bekaa Valley. On 8 June Israeli intelligence examined data from unmanned aerial reconnaissance aircraft and determined that in this region, Syria had deployed 15 2K12 Kub mobile systems and a certain amount of S-125 and S-75 stationary sites with a total of about 200 missiles. They were surrounded by around 400 anti-aircraft guns, including an extremely dangerous ZSU-23-4 vehicles. Most likely there were many Soviets among the personnel. The Soviet Union had equipped Syria with the latest air defence systems[200]. A surprise attack was out of question, because the Syrians had been well aware that the Israeli onslaught was only a matter of time. In two days there would be the biggest air battle since the World War II.

Fighting since June 9

This phase of the battle began on 9 June[201]. First, a number of unmanned aircraft began to fly over the Bekaa Valley, having provided current data on the Syrian forces. They also acted as bait, having forced the Syrian stations to work in the active mode, by which one could recognize their frequencies. Whenever one of the stations turned the radar on, this signal would be immediately intercepted by the E-2C aircraft. The Syrians managed to shoot down a certain number of unmanned

---

[200] I. Rendall, *Splash one: The story…*
[201] The scheme of breaking the Syrian air defence system was published in: J. Gotowała, *Lotnictwo we współczesnych…*, p. 139.

aerial vehicles, but they were relatively cheap (when compared to the aircraft), and in place of one that had been downed, a new one took over its position.

In the second phase, Israel had carried out heavy artillery shelling and launched surface-to-surface missiles, which destroyed the positions of the PLO and some Syrian command posts. The Israeli F-4s, A-4s, F-16s and Kfirs raided the air defence systems with both anti radar AGM-45 Shrike missiles and ordinary bombs. The 2K12 Kub vehicles had not been dug in, which made them easily detectable. In the first strike about 10 were knocked out. By the end of the day destroyed 17 systems of 19 detected were eliminated[202]. The Syrian-Soviet air defence system virtually collapsed on the first day of the fighting[203].

And then the Syrians sent into the air all their fighter aircraft. There was a certain curiosity in this move, unusual and not-reflected in any other conflict, because the fighter planes were deployed to defend the dying ground-based anti aircraft system. It was a reversal of the modern air combat logic, an act of despair and powerlessness[204]. It was a reflexive rather than deliberate reaction[205].

The Israeli unmanned aerial vehicles loitered near the Syrian air bases having recorded takeoff of each aircraft, which was immediately registered by the E-2C airborne command post. Their radars reached deep into Syria and ensured enormous intelligence advantage for their armed forces. The Israeli ECM systems were capable to jam the communications and circulation of any data in almost every Syrian aircraft, thus depriving them of the central command, based on the Soviet model of air defence. In many cases, the Syrians at the start of their mission were deprived of the full control from the ground centres, to depend on which they had been trained. Therefore a number of Syrian fighters entered the battle almost blind.

In contrast, the Israeli E-2Cs, which had dominated as far as information and communications were concerned, with no major problems guided the F-15s and F-16As to the positions optimal for opening fire. Having been aware of the course and altitude of almost any Syrian aircraft, Israeli fighter jets waited for them in the selected position, almost from the moment of takeoff of each of the Syrian MiGs.

On 9 June 1982 over the same are about 150 aircraft clashed (90 Israeli and 60 Syrian)[206] in the biggest air battle since World War II.

---

[202] J. Gotowała, *Lotnictwo we współczesnych...*, p. 138.

[203] I. Rendall, *Splash one: The story...*

[204] *Ibidem.*

[205] In a similar way, during the "war of attrition" the Egyptians were moving their air defence systems closer to the border with the Israel-occupied to hinder the country's aviation operations. This was, in a sense, the act of using anti aircraft systems as a kind of offensive weapons (known is the fact the ground-based anti-aircraft systems are essentially defensive weapons). Out of the defensive system designed to protect Cairo (and not only), they became offensive weapon in this case. See J. Spektor, *Loud and Clear...*

[206] *Ibidem*, p. 215.

From the very beginning the Israeli advantage of information, technology and better training of pilots yielded surprising results. Western sources indicate that on that day Syria lost 22 fighters, and Israel none. The F-15s demonstrated extreme structural strength. There was even a case when a Syrian MiG-21 or MiG-23 hit a F-15 with missile (probably R-3S or R-60), however, the Israeli fighter with one engine switched off managed to return to base. When it had landed, it turned out that apart from the damage caused by the rocket, also had about 400 bullet holes from anti-aircraft gunfire[207]. The Syrians however claimed it had been shot down[208]. The MiGs on the contrary fell to the ground after the first missile had hit them.

The Israeli Air Force had achieved full air supremacy, and the army was advancing further north towards Beirut. The Syrians located additional air defence systems in the Bekaa Valley. They had been quickly detected by the unmanned aircraft, which guided fighting machines. Then, more systems were destroyed.

On the second day, the Syrian air force was still trying to protect the air defence systems and PLO guerillas, but again suffered a defeat. Until the beginning of the third day of fighting, Syria lost some 50 fighters of the original 200 in the region. According to western sources, Israel lost only one aircraft. The culprit was the air defence system[209]. The Israeli troops at all costs wanted to capture Beirut before a truce was signed.

Further pressure of the Israeli troops threatened to break line of communications from Beirut to the Bekaa, so the Syrians once again decided to start the offensive. In these battles they lost another 18 aircraft. By the end of the conflict Syria also lost at least 20 anti-aircraft systems.

Then a ceasefire had been signed, but it was almost immediately broken. Fighting lasted a month, and Syria relocated more air defence systems to the Bekaa consecutive, including newly purchased 9K33 Osa (ZRK Romb, NATO code: SA-8 Gecko). Immediately they had been detected by the UAVs and the aircraft attacked. They destroyed three of the four systems for a loss of one F-4 Phantom and two unmanned aircraft.

The Israeli troops besieged Beirut, Israeli fighter jets, having dominated the airspace over the country, were easily reaching the Lebanese capital and were performing low passes over the city at a supersonic speed. They were also carrying out deceptive approaches to the bombing, to exert psychological pressure on the PLO guerillas. Finally the siege brought resulted in the PLO withdrawal to Tripoli in Tunisia. Task of the operation had been achieved, and on 1 September another ceasefire was signed[210].

---

[207] *Ibidem.*
[208] A. Poray, *Pierwsza…*, Part 2, p. 53.
[209] I. Rendall, *Splash one: The story…*
[210] *Ibidem.*

But the sporadic air skirmishes continued. For example, A. Poray says that on 31 August the Israeli air defense managed to shoot down a reconnaissance MiG-25. It had been first damaged by the MIM-23 Hawk system and then finished off by a F-15. The same source (A. Poray[211]) reports that on 4 October a pair of Syrian MiG-23MSs armed with new R-24 missiles shot down two F-15As, while on 4 December the Syrian MiG-23MLs also shot down one F-15 and one F-4. The Israeli sources have remained silent in both cases.

In February 1983 in the Bekaa Valley the American and French intervened, having performed raids for six days. A. Poray says that Syrian ground-based air defense managed to shoot down three American F-14 Tomcats, one F-4 Phantom, two French Etendards and 11 UAVs[212].

A. Poray also claims that at the turn of October and November 1983 the Syrian S-200 (SA-5 Gammon) missile system shot down an E-2C Hawkeye early warning aircraft. It is not known whether it had belonged to the Israeli or US aviation[213].

On 26 February 1984 the western peacekeeping forces started to withdraw from Lebanon. The process continued until 10 June 1985. And this date is considered as the official end of the so-called First Lebanese War[214]. However, it is rather conventional, since the fighting continued on a limited scale and the state of cold war between Israel and Syria has been continuing to date.

Generally, as part of the operation "Peace for Galilee" the Israeli Air Force carried out more than 2,000 sorties, having officially shot down 85 fighters in air combat (40 shot down by the F-15s, 44 by the F-16As and 1 by an F-4), although some sources say that in fact, this figure may be lower. Over the years it was stresse that the Israeli Air Force in had suffered virtually no losses in the air combat, however, recently some references (eg. articles of A. Poray in "Skrzydlata Polska" published in 2010[215]) indicate that the Syrian MiG-21s and MiG-23s managed to shoot down few Israeli machines during the conflict (including an F-16A), although undoubtedly the Syrians suffered a crushing defeat. Interestingly, over the Bekaa Valley in 1982 Syria did not use its latest assets – the MiG-25Ps. One can only guess that after two such exceptionally expensive aircraft had been lost in combat against the F-15, it was decided to save these machines and perhaps limit their role to defend the capital and intercept reconnaissance aircraft over Syria itself.

Once again AIM-9L missiles (which can be also fired at a target from the front hemisphere), proved to be much more effective in maneuvering air combat than the Soviet R-3S or even the newer R-60. In addition, the Israeli Air Force used the

---

[211] A. Poray, *Pierwsza...*, Part 2, p. 55.
[212] *Ibidem.*
[213] *Ibidem.*
[214] *Ibidem.*
[215] The series of articles was published in "Skrzydlata Polska" Issue Nos. 2/2010, 3/2010 and 4/2010.

Shafrir missiles produced at home and the latest Python III. Once again, almost no medium-range missiles were used (AIM-7F, R-23R/T), and even if they had been fired, it was usually done to cause the aforementioned "hit the cauldron" effect[216].

In total, 93% of air victories in this conflict had been won with missiles and only 7% with by gunfire[217].

The Israeli side scored a much higher number of kills than the Syrians, but to determine the exact number of downed aircraft is impossible. Both sides overstate enemy losses and understate their own. According to most Israeli and American sources, the Israeli fighter aircraft shot down about 80–88 MiGs, without any losses in the air combat[218]. Russian/Soviet and Syrian reports claim that Israel lost 23 fighter jets in air combat and another 27 downed by the ground based systems. Additionally, according to the same sources, the Syrians were supposed to shoot down 3 helicopters and 7 unmanned aerial vehicles. Syria admitted it had lost 67–68 aircraft (including 51–57 downed by the Israeli fighters, 4 crashed because lack of fuel or damage and 7–12 eliminated by Israel's air defence). The Syrians also record a loss of 18 Gazelle helicopters[219]. Some victories were very problematic. Generally speaking, the exact calculation of losses of both sides of the conflict (as well as most other conflicts) is virtually impossible.

Conclusions from the war in Lebanon in 1982 had been drawn throughout the world. As a result, the Soviet Union even formed a special secret commission to explain what had been the cause of these extremely high losses. This conflict clearly showed that the party in possession of significant amount of information can use a relatively small number of aircraft and highly trained pilots to achieve victory over centrally controlled, virtually inflexible Soviet system (a kind of "colossus on the feet of clay"), where the destruction of command centres, or at least jamming communication with them the fighter aircraft pilots become almost blind. There were also some mental limitations of this system – the pilots had been trained in the eastern methodology eastern and were only following orders from command posts. Their own individual creativity had been restricted to a minimum or even persecuted. As a result, the pilot (eg. the Syrian, Egyptian or Soviet), after he had lost contact

---

[216] J. Gotowała, *Lotnictwo we współczesnych...*, p. 140.

[217] I. Rendall, *Splash one: The story...*

[218] According to western sources, 48 of them were shot down by the F-15s and the rest by the F-16s. See: J. Gruszczyński, E. F. Rybak, *F-15 Eagle*, ed. Magnum-X, Warsaw, 2001, p. 50 and M. Fisher, J. Gruszczyński, *F-16 Jastrząb*, ed. Magnum-X, Warsaw, 2006, p. 111. Score of about 80 Syrian aircraft (including 36 MiG-23s) and 2 Israeli machines is given in *MiG-23MF*, collective work, ed. Altair, Warsaw, 1992, p. 25 and *MiG-23 wersje myśliwskie*, collective work, ed. Magnum-X, Warsaw, 1999, p. 73.

[219] A. Poray, *Pierwsza...*, Part 3, p. 50. According to the Soviet data, the most air victories of the Syrian side were achieved by the MiG-21s, which were to shoot down 5 F-15s, 1 F-16, 2 F-4s, 2 A-4s, 1 Kifir and 6 unidentified aircraft. The Syrian MiG-23s were to shoot down 5 F-16s and two F-4s. The Western references fiercely criticised this information, having considered them fabrication of the Soviet propaganda. See: Ibid, p. 51.

with the command, not only did not see anything and did not know what to do, but even he was afraid to decide his own fate (in a sense it was the aftermath of the 19th century views that the soldier was supposed to fear of his superior more than his opponent, which were promoted widely in the Soviet Union and Eastern Bloc countries). The Syrian pilots, after their chain of command had been incapacitated, did not receive orders to return to base, so still flew on to fight the enemy who was trained better than them and equipped with a much more modern equipment. In most cases, the MiGs had got hit by the missiles before they noticed the presence of the enemy. In fact, almost identical conclusions could have been drawn already from earlier conflicts (1967 and 1973). However, in Moscow they had ignored them, which caused defeats of the countries equipped in the Soviet manner and thus implemented eastern methods of fighting[220]. Dissenting voices were few. For example, a Soviet air force analyst Colonel Vasily Dubrov, in a note to the Soviet Ministry of Defence, described the Israeli measures electronic warfare, modern guided missiles and early warning E-2Cs, as the "wave of the future", having praised the Israeli methodology of organization and use of aviation[221]. This did not, however, influenced a policy of training in his homeland.

It is worth noting what American intelligence thought at that time of the Warsaw Pact pilots (especially from the USSR) as well as the allies of the East[222]: *The level of training of Soviet fighter pilots were very diverse. The best pilots of the best fighter regiments matched their western counterparts[223], but in various regiments or even within the same regiment heterogeneous criteria were applied, which generally lowered to the level of the least able individuals – an inherent feature of the Soviet system of selection and training of pilots, which was sluggish, bureaucratic, inflexible, subordinated to ideology and prone to abuse. (…) the candidates were required perfect physical and mental health, as well as adequate education* (which in fact had been won in a similar methodology – JM), *but seniority in the communist party was also taken into account the and recommendation from the party was always helpful, so conformism had become the personal skills and predispositions. The approach to combat training was completely different than in the West: after four years of study and basic training a new pilot was*

---

[220] In fact, the only country that widely bought military equipment in the USSR, but used a Western philosophy of training and fighting, was Finland. Mentally and politically belonged to the West, but was forced to buy large quantities of equipment (eg. MiG-21) in the Soviet Union for political reasons (having financed in this way the Soviet industry with hard to obtain western currency).

[221] I. Rendall, *Splash one: The story...*

[222] *Ibidem*, pp. 199–200.

[223] Polish pilot Ryszard Obacz who in 1963 fled to the West on a TS-8 Bies plane and then worked for military intelligence DIA says that the level of aviation training, he had received in the Polish air force equalled the Western one: *When I had been promoted I was sent me to my first line unit and felt fully prepared for the next stage of education – combat training. Today I know that we did not need to be ashamed when compared to our contemporary colleagues from NATO. We knew more about the techniques of piloting and air combat tactics and if necessary we would fight them effectively.* Source: R. Kowal, *Rozmowy...*, p. 23.

assigned straight to one of the regiments of aviation as a lieutenant and only there he was undergoing actual training. If senior officers had been good pilots and instructors, the newcomers were placed high demands, and if not, the level was lowered. Western air forces conducted such training in specialized centres where a high level was maintained, and weaker students dropped out. (...) The Soviet pilot had to assimilate a huge amount of theoretical material before he began combat training that consisted in the repetitions of established procedures, responding to every hypothetical tactical situation but not of development of own initiative and the ability to cope with unforeseen dangers. When more enlightened senior commanders of the Soviet air force had rebuked the unit leaders that pilots should have been taught greater independence, it turned out that it was very difficult to develop initiative and self-confidence in a disciplined society, where the stiffness of ideas and conformity of thought were recognized virtues and ways to achieve promotion.

As we can see, it was very difficult to change such an attitude in the Soviet Union. It looked quite similar or even identical in the Warsaw Pact countries and among other allies of the USSR of similar authoritarian social and political systems, including Egypt, Syria or Iraq. As early as in 1972 the Soviet high command realized that mental limitations described above hindered to take advantage of all features of the latest MiG-25 fighter. If it had been piloted by an experienced pilot trained in western methodology, its combat capabilities would be much greater. This construction was far more advanced than its predecessors, ahead of the Soviet society civilization. However, due to the contemporary level of social development, the role of the MiG-25, out of necessity had to be restricted to the "airborne anti-aircraft post", although on its base a versatile, autonomous, multi-role battle machine could have been developed, similar to the F-14 Tomcat. This peculiar situation with the MiG-25s is being described by I. Rendall[224]: *In the early 70's the senior commanders of the Soviet air force realized with painful clarity that changing world of military aviation also required a thorough reconstruction of the principles of pilot training and at the core of any changes in the way of thinking, had to be the issue of increasing independence of fighter pilot. Soviet doctrine for decades had relied on a system of ground control and the MiG-25 was designed according to the principle that "modus operanti" did not allow for pilot's independent action. This "passive" approach had permeated the Soviet mentality and way of training their pilots. Training still consisted of repeating rigid procedures, and not on developing individual skills and the will to fight, which was required by a new defence doctrine (...).*

This problem had even deepened with the introduction of next-generation fighters, such as MiG-29 and Su-27[225]. The Russians have failed to solve this problem

---

[224] I. Rendall, *Splash one: The story...*
[225] *Ibidem*, p. 201.

properly to date. The same reasons contributed to the disaster and the enormous losses of the Arab states fighting with Israel. This was, among others, the case of Syria, whose fighters (even modern and very dangerous MiG-25Ps), were unable to defeat the enemy – relatively small number of modern-trained pilots centres backed by the most modern western production technology. The combination of western mentality and training methods having derived from this style and the state-of-the-art fighter (especially F-15), produced the most effective air force.

While describing the conflict over the Bekaa Valley it should be noted that it had been fought with standard equipment of NATO and the Warsaw Pact air forces. Both blocs tested their doctrines and the equipment by sending it to the Middle East, along with advisers. The eastern and western views on the air forces were applied there, but mostly on tactical or operational level. There was massive invasion of Arab land forces in 1973. In case of this conflict even the Syrians had assumed that the main means of combat would be the air defence, i.e. Fighter aircraft and ground-based systems, which was a departure from the Warsaw Pact doctrines which had focused on operations by the masses of ground troops, supported only by the air force.

2.5. Other dogfights involving the Air Force of Israel

After the battles over Lebanon in 1982 the Israeli Air Force took part in a series of military operations against the Lebanese and Palestinian factions. No air combat occurred, because the opponents did not have any aviation. In 1978 Egypt ended the dispute with Israel and signed the agreement at Camp David and the fighting between the planes of those countries would never again happen. Smaller Arab states also significantly reduced their share in the fight against Israel, or virtually withdrew from the conflict. The only major adversary of Israel was still Syria, on the border of which from time to time to various incidents and provocations took place. Complete knowledge of the subject is still not available, because both sides do not reveal details of such operations.

From time to time only in the aviation-related publications or Internet[226] reports appear on sporadic air combat between the Syrian and Israeli air forces which sup-

---

[226] Article on the subject was published – among others – by one of the most famous websites on ACIG air combat: T. Cooper, Israeli-Syrian Shadow-Boxing., ACIG, 30 September 2003; http://www.acig. info/CMS/ and Israel downed two Syrian MIGs in 2001 WorldTribune.com, 2005 http://www.worldtribune. com/worldtribune/05/breaking2453413.05625.html.

The author of the article (Tom Cooper) is a well known author of numerous publications on the air wars after World War II. During the many years of research the author has gained many contacts in the Middle East, therefore his studies on the air forces of the Arab countries contain a lot of information and photographs published for the first time. The most famous publications of T. Cooper are: T. Cooper, F. Bishop, *Iranian F-14 Tomcat Units in Combat*, Oxford, UK, 2004; T. Cooper, N. Nicolle, *Arab MiG-19 and MiG-21 Units in Combat…*; T. Cooper, F. Bishop, *Iran-Iraq War in the Air 1980–1988*, ed. Shiffer, 2003;

posedly occurred at the turn of the twentieth and twenty-first century. Note, however, that the information have not been confirmed by the Israeli government and should be approached with caution.

For example on 2 June 1989 two Israeli F-15Cs probably shot down two Syrian MiG-29s[227] in unknown circumstances. Another similar skirmish supposedly took place on 14 September 2001 When another two Syrian MiG-29s was shot down by a pair of the Israeli F-15Cs. The first MiG was reportedly hit by the Python Mk.IV missile, and the second one by the AIM-9M. The MiGs were about to intercept an Israeli reconnaissance aircraft flying near the coastline of Lebanon. This incident has not been officially confirmed by Israeli nor Syrian sources. There is also information that in 1990 a Syrian pilot escaped on a MiG-29 fighter to Israel, where the plane was to be tested in 1991[228] (later, in 1997 Israel tested 2–3 MiG-29 on loan from Poland[229]).

The well-known website site that describes the ACIG air combat also says that in April 2002 a Syrian MiG-23 shot with a guided missile an Israeli unmanned aerial vehicle, which was heading the Syrian town of al-Suwayda. The incident took place about 100 km north of the Jordanian city of Amman. The Syrian radars detected during this time increased air traffic of Jordanian helicopters near the border. Their most probable task to take over the Israeli UAV (perhaps also from the Syrian territory). The Syrian group on a Mi-8 helicopter, however, was faster and captured the wreckage. Presumably from this reason the Israelis suspended the UAV missions over Syria for some time.

Although between Israel and Syria since the 90' there has been no state of war, the two sides conducted the increased observation of border regions by air reconnaissance. T. Cooper says also that a few years ago, a major of the Syrian air force revealed in an interview that: *Every year, between eight and nine reconnaissance missions were performed along the border with Israel, and sometimes even deeper into Israeli territory. These operations have been ignored by Israel.*

---

four parts of the monograph *Arab MIGs* and T. Cooper, A. Sadik, *Iraqi Fighters: 1953–2003: Camouflage and markings*, ed. Harpy, 2008.

[227] T. Cooper says that in 2000–2001 Syria received 16 MiG-29 fighters, which were probably machines originally intended for Iraq, built in 1990–1991 and subsequently modernized. Earlier, in the late 80's Syria had already received 48 MiG-29/MiG-29UB aircraft and the first Syrian unit equipped with them was 697th Squadron from Tsaykal, led by Maj. al-Masry – pilot who shot down an Israeli F-4 Phanom on 9 October 1982 (another Syrian pilot of the same name shot down two Israeli planes in 1974 on a MiG-23). Later the MiG-29s were supplied to 698th and 699th Squadron – both stationed at Tsaykal. Yefim Gordon says that the first MiG-29 arrived to Syria in July 1987, the first squadron was operational in October 1988 and not more than 80 (out of 150 ordered) had been delivered to Syria, including 48 in the late 80s Y. Gordon, *Mikoyan MiG-29*, ed. Midland, Hinckley, United Kingdom, 2006, p. 500.

[228] Y. Gordon, *Mikoyan MiG-29*, pp. 485 and 500.

[229] The amount of two MiG-29s on loan from the Polish is given by Y. Gordon, *Mikoyan MiG-29…*, p. 483, while M. Bogdański in the article *MiG-29 w Polsce*, in "Aeroplan" Issue No. 5–6 / 2006, Special edition – monograph of the MiG-29) on p. 13, says that in 1997 Israel received three Polish MiG-29s serial numbers 105, 114 and 115 (see Chapter I).

In another interview a Syrian colonel repeated the information and added: *It is routine for the Syrian air defense system radars that they monitored the movements of Israeli reconnaissance aircraft over northern Israel, Lebanon and the Golan region. The same applies to the Israeli radars when Syrian reconnaissance planes operate along the borders with Israel.* The colonel is also said that none of the parties did not open fire, even in case the reconnaissance aircraft of opposite side had been intercepted.

Since the late 80's, a few times the Israeli and Syrian aircraft have been approaching very close to each other but did not open fire. A Syrian reserve officer and former operator of Kub (SA-6) anti-aircraft system described one of the encounters: *As a rule, we only track the enemy reconnaissance aircraft on a radar, but do not open fire. They do the same thing. When we were in an advanced camp in the region of Golan in 1996 we observed our aircraft as well as theirs having approached each other at a very small distance and then – at a certain imaginary line – both sides turned back. Sometimes the aircraft of both sides exceed this line, but never there was any reaction of the opponent. This was done directly over the occupied Golan region, but outside the actual territory of Israel.*

In the 90s the Syrian MiG-25R/RBs were carrying out regular reconnaissance flights near the borders with Israel, and sometimes deep into enemy territory. It is estimated that about 2010 the Syrian air force still flied two MiG-25RBs attached to the 7th OCU at the Shayrat air base and to the 9th Squadron from Dmeyr. To perform the flights in the vicinity of Israel (or over the country), they were transferred to al-Ladhiqiyah.

In the early summer of 2001 the Israelis, however, changed the procedure and commenced both aircraft and UAV reconnaissance missions deep over the Syrian territory. In mid-July of this year, two Israeli fighter jets flew over Syria and headed to Halab (Aleppo). The Syrians sent into the air a pair of MiG-29s fighters and a pair of MiG-25s, which intercepted Israeli planes over Idlib, about 35 km from the Turkish border. Then the Israeli fighters turned back and went away in the direction of the Syrian coastline on the Mediterranean Sea, where the Syrian radars detected movements of at least 12 Israeli aircraft. The Syrian government took an immediate decision to not start fighting and all the MiGs returned to their bases.

On 27 July 2001 a pair of Israeli fighters appeared again over Syria, now from direction of Turkey at a high altitude. The Israelis again flew over Idlib, and then set a course on al-Ladhiqiyah (Latakia). During the flight over Ash-Shughur, about 30 km southwest of Idlib, they were detected by Kub (SA-6) system, which had been located in the area recently. This forced the Israeli group to change course. The Syrian fighters took off and the Israeli formation turned and left the territory of Syria, then flew along the border with Turkey and eventually in the international air space over the Mediterranean Sea.

The situation escalated even more after the terrorist attack on New York in 2001. Both sides began to look at each other with even greater suspicion. On 14 September 2001 a Boeing 707 of the Israeli Air Force equipped with reconnaissance equipment (SIGINT) performed reconnaissance flight along the coastline of Lebanon and nearby Syrian territory.

It was collecting electronic data, especially from the region Tarabulus and Hamidiye. The Boeing was flying at a speed of 520 knots at an altitude of 30,000 feet and was escorted by two F-15Cs armed the latest air-to-air Python Mk.IV missiles. The Israeli aircraft had been performing such flights about twice a week for some time. A pair of Syrian fighters on duty took off. Usually these were the MiG-23s from Abu ad-Duhor or MiG-29s from Tsaykal, which had been transferred to al-Ludhiqiyah to be closer to the Mediterranean. The Syrian fighters always kept about 20 km from the Israeli formation and did not demonstate will to attack.

But on that day at 09.14 hrs two MiG-29s had been sent to intercept the Israeli B707 and suddenly performed a turn in the direction of the Israeli formation at increased speed. Pilots of the Israeli F-15s understood this move as preparation to attack. The MiGs were constantly approaching at high speed and at any time were capable to open fire. The commander of a pair of the F-15s immediately ordered the B707 to withdraw from this area, to enable the ECM and asked the ground-based command post for support. As a result of this request more aircraft took off – 6 F-15s, 6 F-16s and a tanker (a Boeing 707).

Then the commander of the Israeli formation gave warning to the Syrians to change the coursethe international emergency frequency. It has not been known whether the Syrians received this message. With no response or reaction on their part, the Israeli fighter jets headed toward the MiGs. The first F-15 attacked a MiG from the front hemisphere from above, coming out of the sun and hit it with the infrared guided missile Python Mk.IV launched at an angle of 40 degrees beyond the infrared beam point. It was the first time the Python Mk.IV missile was launched in anger. The second MiG-29 immediately bounced back strongly to the right, probably turning over Syria, but it was also intercepted. A F-15 launched the AIM-9M missile from a distance only 500 m and downed the second MiG. Its flaming debris fell into the sea. Both Syrian pilots (Maj. Arshad Midhat Mubarak and Capt. Ahmad al-Khatab) managed to eject and were rescued by a Syrian ship. The names of the Israeli pilots involved in this fight are still classified information. Then both sides (Syrian and Israeli) attempted to conceal the incident. The Syrians were reluctant to inform of the action, where they were defeated, and Israel was then focused on the conflict with the Palestinians. The Israeli government kept silence, while the Syrian government denied everything. Minister of Foreign Affairs of Syria issued a statement then: *Yes, the Syrian air force had a serious emergency situation in the air on that day in the air, but as far as I know, no aircraft had been lost.*

After this incident, Israel temporarily cancelled flights in the area. In April 2002 over Syria appeared the Israeli unmanned aerial vehicles and commenced regular flights until one of them was shot down. At that time, neither party was interested escalation of the conflict. The new president of Syria B. Assad was busy at strengthening his power, while Israel had enough problems related to the activities of the Palestinians in the West Bank and Gaza Strip.

Presumably, the entire event had been caused by too nervous pilots (first the Syrians and then the Israelis, who were provoked to open fire in self-defence) and not due to the high command orders.

There is a possibility that the activity of the Israeli Air Force reconnaissance aircraft during that period was focused on observation of the vessels sailing to Syrian ports, especially al-Ladhiqiyah and Tarabulus. Some of the shipping could have contained arms for Iraq – two such cases had been discovered in February 2002 but there was possibility that they would be repeated. Undoubtedly, after the cargo had been unloaded it was expected to observe increased land traffic in Syria. Perhaps the Israeli UAV shot down over Syria in April 2002 by a MiG-23 was looking for it. The Israeli reconnaissance operations were probably secretly backed by Jordan.

There is also a possibility that the Israeli Air Force operations were related to suspicions that Syria could have worked on development of its own mass destruction weapons[230], including nuclear technology. As in case of Iraq, the possession of an atomic bomb by Syrian regime was a huge threat to Israel and to the entire civilized world. Israel took this threat very seriously and, consequently, the Israeli Air Force raided the likely Syrian nuclear reactor in 2007 (see previous section of the book).

---

[230] In July 2007 there was an explosion in Aleppo, in northern Syria. The official news agency Sana reported 15 people killed among the Syrian military personnel and another 50 wounded. The Agency said that the cause of the explosion was a fire, which reached flammable products stored in the facility. According to reports of the "Jane's Defence Weekly" the cause of the explosion was a failed test launch of the Scud C missile (the R-17 variant with a range of 500–600 km and 600 kg warhead, accuracy 700 m from the aiming point) filled with mustard gas. See: *Syria blast, linked to chemical weapons' report*, Agence France-Presse (AFP), 19.09.2007.

Yom Kippur War of 1973

The Yom Kippur War battlefield

The Israeli Mirage III with two air combat kill markings

The Egyptian S-125 Neva (SA-3 Goa) anti-aircraft ground missile system

The Israeli A-4 Skyhawk

The Egyptian Tu-16 bomber
aircraft, some of them
armed with the KSR-2/AS-5
Kelt missiles

The US F-8 intercepting an Egyptian Tu-16, May 1969

The Egyptian Su-7BM ground attack fighter jet

The Egyptian MiG-21MF. Perhaps one of the machines flown by the pilots of the Soviet 135th Fighter Aircraft Regiment, Beni Suef 1970

Some patrol routes of the Soviet MiG-25R/RB recce aircraft of the 63. Independent Air Unit

Dassault Mirage IIICJ – 101 Squadron Israeli Defence Force 1967

Dassault Mirage IIICJ – 101 Squadron Israeli Defence Force 1970

Dassault Mirage IIICJ – 101 Squadron Israeli Defence Force 1970

McDonnell-Douglas F-4E – 119 Squadron Israeli Defence Force 1973

Mikoyan-Gurevich MiG-21F-13 – Egyptian Air Force 1967

Mikoyan-Gurevich MiG-21PFM – Egyptian Air Force (UAR) 1970

Mikoyan-Gurevich MiG-21PFM – Syrian Air Force 1972

Mikoyan-Gurevich MiG-21R – Egyptian Air Force 1973

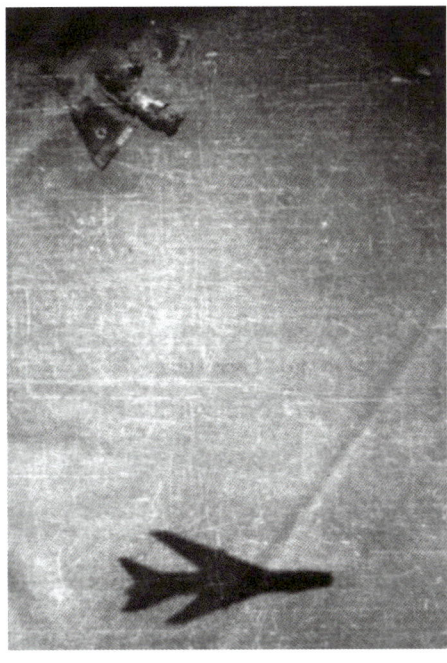

The Israeli A-4Es tail end. The aircraft was downed during the Yom Kippur War

The Egyptian Su-7 flying over the bombed Refidim airbase (wreckage of an Israeli Mirage or Nesher can be seen in the background)

The IAF F-4 Phantom on display at Hatzerim Muzeum

The Israeli MQM-74 Chucar (Telem) flying target. Many of them were flown over enemy territory to multiply quantity of the potential targets for the ground based AA systems which would thus reveal their location

The Egyptian Il-28U bomber-trainer

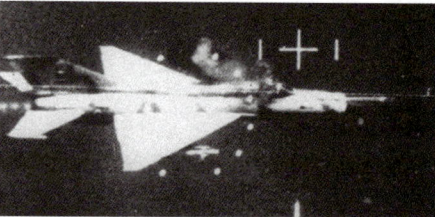

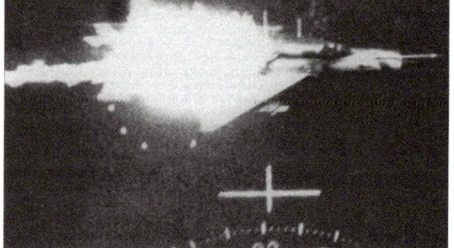

The Egyptian MiG-17F

The Egyptian MiG-21PFM being hit by an
air-to-air missile

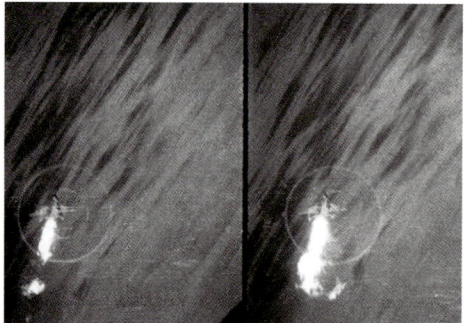

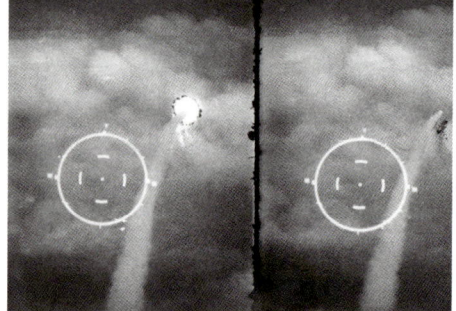

Another Egyptian MiG being hit

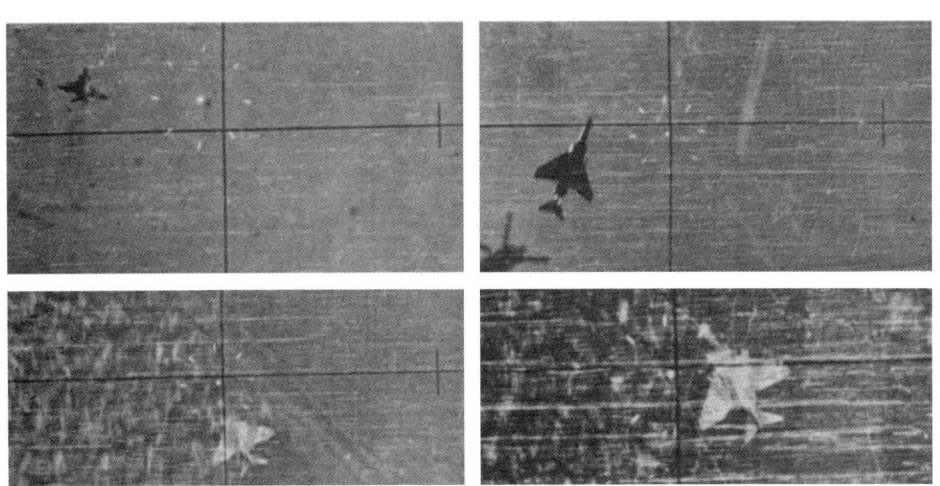

The Israeli F-4 Phantom in the MiGs sights

Arab MiG-21 as seen from the Israeli fighter

Operation "Peace for Galilee",
the Bekaa Valley (Lebanon) 1982

The tail parts of Su-7 and MiG-19 on display at Hatzerim

The Soviet S-75 (SA-2) ground based AA system as used by both Egypt and Syria

The shot down Su-7, most likely in 1973

The tail part of a Syrian MiG-23 downed over the Bekaa Valley in 1982

The Syrian MiG-21bis fighter jets (present photographs)

The Syrian
MiG-23MF
in a sheltered
hangar (present
photographs)

The R-13M
(AA-2C Advanced
Atoll) air-to-air
missiles, armament
of the Syrian
MiG-21bis and
MiG-23MF aircraft.
It was a Soviet
equivalent of the
AIM-9G Sidewinder
(present photograph)

The Syrian
R-60 and R-23
missiles, the Syrian
MiG-23s armament
(present photograph)

The Syrian Mi-8
helicopters
(present photograph)

The Syrian 2K12 Kub (SA-6 Gainful) launcher vehicle at the Israeli museum.

The Syrian MiG-17F preserved at the Aleppo University. In 1982 these obsolete aircraft performed ground attack missions

Riyadh Ali Hmesheh and his MiG-17F No. 1219, killed in action over Lebanon in 1982

The Syrian MiG-23ML (present photograph)

The Syrian MiG-21MF/bis and MiG-23BN/MiG-27 aircraft firing the S-24 unguided missiles (present photograph)

The IAF Grumman E-2C Hawkeye early warning aircraft

The IAI Scout UAV. These machines proved to be very useful in locating the Syrian radar sites and ground-based air defence systems

The Israeli F-15A with two kill markings

The Israeli marking painted on the aircraft which had destroyed the Syrian AA systems in 1982

A knocked out Syrian T-62 on the road near Jezzine, 8 June 1982 and a heavily damaged Israeli Merkava. Its commander, Tzur Maor, managed to hit six Syrian T-62s before he was mortally wounded. The Syrian losses on the ground were as much heavy as in the air

The Israeli A-4 Skyhawks

The Israeli F-16B. The multi-role F-16 is a rare example when two-seater variant retains full combat capabilities, virtually the same as a one-seater. In most types of aircraft combat capabilities of the two-seaters are, in fact quite limited when compared to the basic models. Subsequent specialized Israeli variant F-16I Sufa is actually only a two-seater version

The IAI Kfir and a full set of its armament at the Hatzerim museum

The Israeli A-4 Skyhawk being armed

The IAF RF-4 Phantom reconnaissance aircraft

The Israeli F-4 Phantom

Other dogfights involving the Air Force of Israel

The Israeli F-16Cs performing combat mission
[3D Visualisation by Graham Gazzard, model 3D Anders Lejczak]

The F-16I Sufa – one of the most modern combat aircraft these days

A flight of Israeli F-16I Sufa aircraft

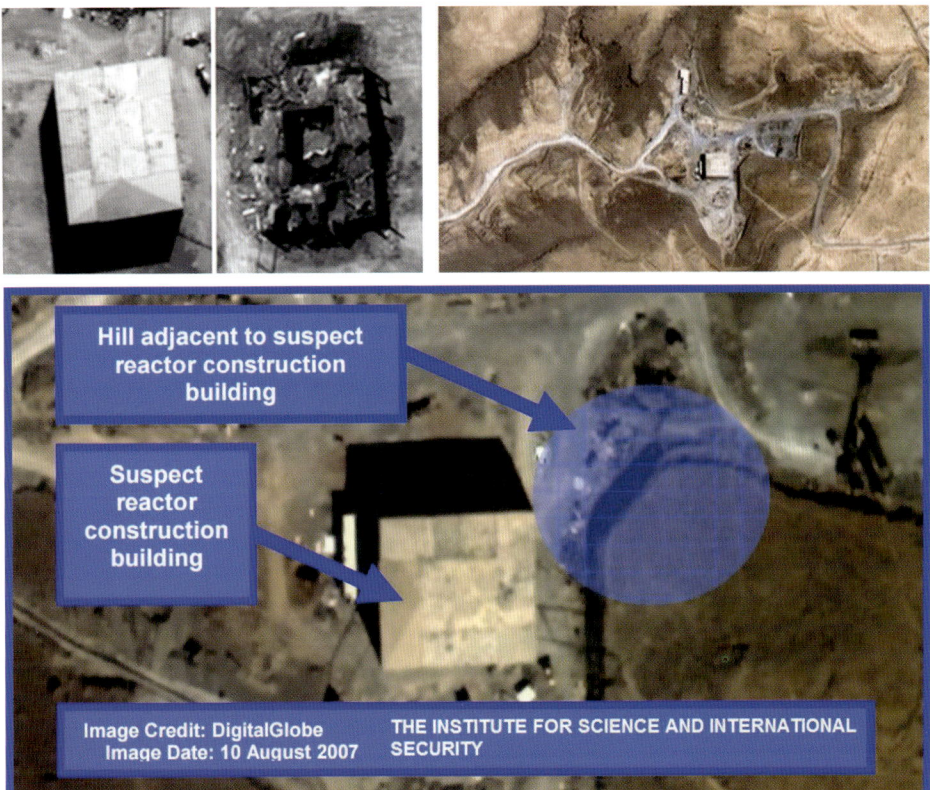

The possible Syrian nuclear reactor site before and after the air-strike of 6 September 2007

The 69th Squadrons F-15I refuelling from a Boeing 707 tanker aircraft

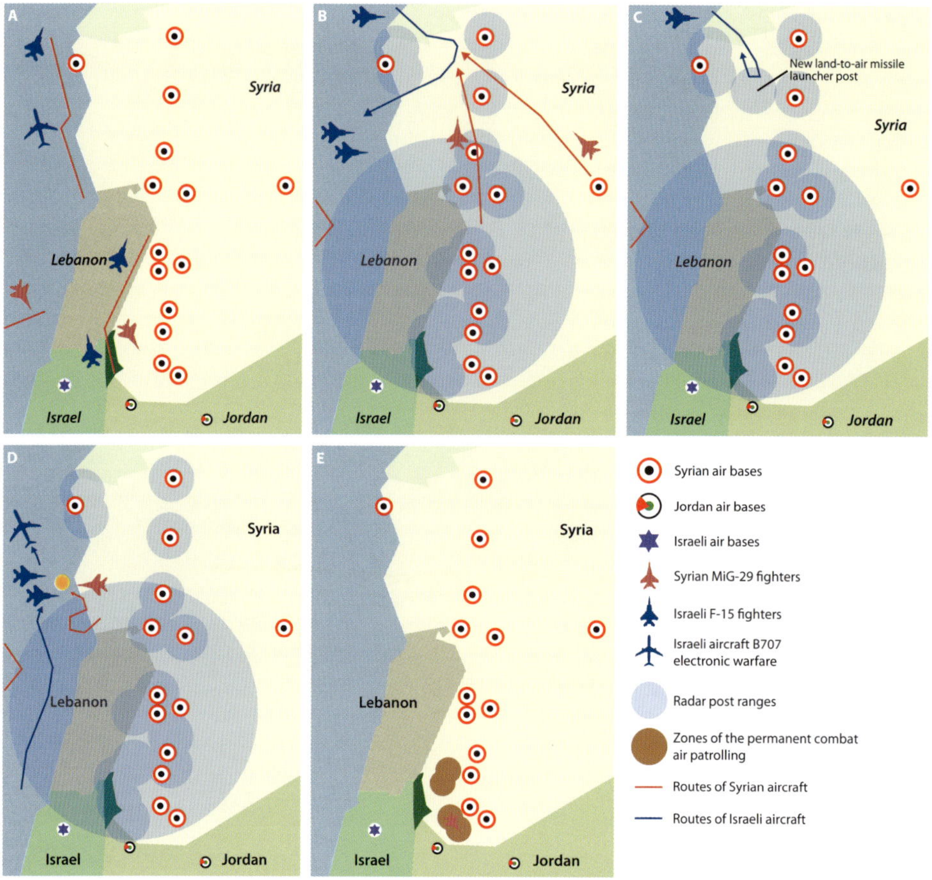

Legend:
- Syrian air bases
- Jordan air bases
- Israeli air bases
- Syrian MiG-29 fighters
- Israeli F-15 fighters
- Israeli aircraft B707 electronic warfare
- Radar post ranges
- Zones of the permanent combat air patrolling
- Routes of Syrian aircraft
- Routes of Israeli aircraft

(Map labels: A, B, C, D, E — Syria, Lebanon, Israel, Jordan; "New land-to-air missile launcher post")

The likely course of events in the air space over Israel, Lebanon and Syria at the turn of the twentieth and twenty-first century. A – the situation in the 1990's, when none of the parties does not exceed the red lines or opened fire himself; B – July 2001., Israeli recce aircraft (probably RF-4E and F-16/F-15) coming in from over Turkey. They are intercepred over Idlib and turn back to the Mediterranean. About 12 Israeli fighter aircraft waiting at the ready, to give them support them; C – 27 July 2001 Israeli recce aircraft re-enters Syria from over Turkey, but returns after it had been tracked by a new station Kub (SA-6) system located at Jisr ash-Shughur; D – 14 September 2001, Israeli F-15 shot down a pair of Syrian MiG-29s; E – April 2002. Syrian MiG-23 shoots down an Israeli unmanned air vehicle in one of the zones of permanent combat patrolling in the air (brown-coloured areas on the map) near the border with Jordan [drawn according to: T. Cooper, Israeli-Syrian Shadow-Boxing]

The IAF 69th Squadron „The Hammers" insignia

The F-15I Raam, 69th Squadron IAF

Painted by Bill Dady

Lockheed-Martin F-16A Block 10 – 253 Squadron Israeli Defence Force 1980

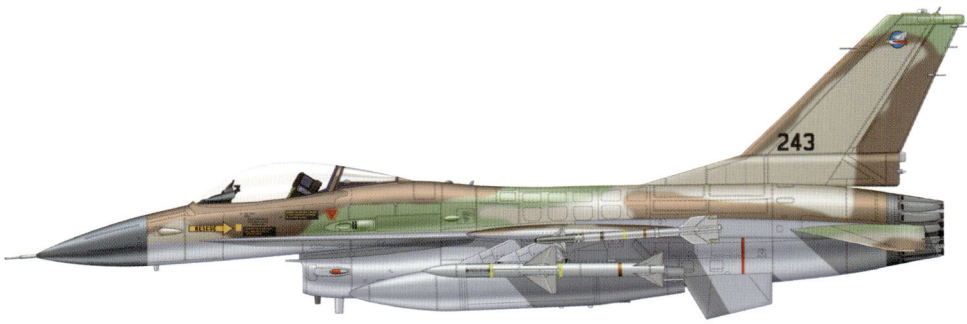

Lockheed-Martin F-16A Block 10 – 110 Squadron Israeli Defence Force 1981

Painted by Bill Dady

Lockheed-Martin F-16A Block 5
– 117 Squadron Israeli Defence Force 1982

Mikoyan-Gurevich MiG-29B
– 699 Squadron Syrian Air Force 1998

Lockheed-Martin F-16A Block 10
– 116 Squadron Israeli Defence Force 2000

Lockheed-Martin F-16A Block 10
– 140 Squadron Israeli Defence Force 2000

Lockheed-Martin F-16A Block 10
– 115 Squadron Israeli Defence Force 2010

The Israeli F-15 – close up view of its armament

The Syrian MiG-29 aircraft

The underwing Python Mk. IV missile and the IAF F-15

The Syrian MiG-23 at the Hama airbase during the present civil war. This would have been looked actually the same back in the 1980's

The newest IAF's acquisition – a Lockheed Martin F-35I Adir during its maiden flight on 13 December 2016

Conclusion

The conflict between Israel and the Arab world has been continuing with varying intensity for a long time and there is no clear perspective of its final solution. Although Israel does not fight openly with Egypt, Syria is concentrated on its own civil war, but the Arab world is still strongly antagonized with the Jewish State. Israel has won its independence during the War of 1948 and strengthened and maintained it by defeating the armies of the Arab states (mainly Egypt and Syria) in a number of successive conflicts, which are de facto the elements of a sustainable war, which has been stretching throughout at least twentieth century.

In each of these conflicts very large or even decisive role was played by the aviation. Ironically, it was Israel that has shown the world a perfect example of "Blitzkrieg" – sudden unexpected strikes annihilated air forces of Egypt and Syria during the Six Day War 1967. Later the same scheme was largely repeated during the Yom Kippur War in 1973.

In 1967 Israeli and Arab states were comparable as far as technology was concerned. Israel won due flexible command system and better training of personnel (especially pilots). Later, since the supplies of American F-4 Phantom in the '70s, the Israeli Air Force began to increasingly exceed the Arab states technologically.

The technological advantage of Israel over the Arab states had become even more devastating when in the 80's the US delivered the F-16s and F-15s to Israel. The newest MiG-23, MiG-25 and MiG-29 fighters, supplied at this time to Syria from the Soviet Union, were no match for the most recent Israeli aircraft

The key to victory of the Israeli aviation was not only the most modern technology, but also incomparably better command and training, as well as mental issues. Israel is a country representing largely western mentality, where a large role is played by the idea of personal freedom and the creative thinking. Therefore, the Israeli officer, including the pilot, could in certain situations personally make decisions that theoretically exceeded his competences[231]. The Israeli armed forces from the beginning have rewarded independent thinking and unconventional action. This

---

[231] See J. Spektor, *Loud and Clear...*

was to be the force of thinking people, not "robots" mechanically performing each command, without attempting to think outside the imposed level.

In the Arab forces Soviet mental model had dominated, which eliminated the individual thinking, and every soldier and officer had only mechanically to perform imposed orders, thinking turned off. These armies were not only massive, but also not flexible and worked according to pre-imposed scheme. Practice has shown that such a "colossus with feet of clay" could be defeated by a much less numerous armed forces, equipped with modern technology and above all well-trained, with huge motivation to fight and flexible mental model – like the mythical David defeated Goliath.

The Israeli-Arab wars are still the subject of many discussions, articles, publications, websites and excite the imagination of modelling fraternity. On the web one can find numerous photos of realistic models of military equipment, which took part in the battles described in this book.

From the point of view of international security alarming is the fact that the Middle East is still not a safe place. Several decades have passed, but the region is still full of hatred and mutual grievances on the territorial, economic, cultural and religious grounds. This also applies to Israel and its surroundings. The question of the borders of the Jewish state is still not accepted by the Arab nations. Although at present Egypt no longer undertakes any military action against Israel, and Syria is engulfed by civil war and has no forces to oppose Israel, but no one is able to rule out escalation of violence in the future. That is why, even today, in the twenty-first century the Israeli armed forces together with its aviation constantly acquires most modern combat equipment (including multi-purpose combat aircraft F-35) and ensures the highest level of training for the personnel. The former main enemy – Egypt – tries to follow the same path, although financial constraints and the policy of this country do not permit such a modern army like Israel. It is known, however, that Egypt bought recently in Russia a batch of the MiG-29M fighters and Mi-28 assault helicopters, France delivered a number of modern Rafale fighters and also Mistral assault ships designed originally for Russia.

As we can see, the Middle East states continue to "baring their teeth at each other", and the peace is being maintained largely by the kind of balance (or rather race) of arms caused by a further escalation of violence, which this region has been experiencing over the past few years.

Selected bibliography

Publications

Aloni S., *Arab-Israeli air wars 1947–1982,* Osprey, UK, 2001

Ball R., *The Israeli Air Force Part One 1948 to 1967,* Guideline Publications, UK, 2000.

Ball R., *Camuflage & markings – the Israeli Air Force, Part Two: 1967 to 2001,* Guideline Publications, UK, 2001.

Bartosik S., Łaz M., Senkowski R., *MiG-21F-13 w służbie polsko-syryjskiej* in: "Lotnictwo", Issue No. 12/2008.

Bar-Zohar M., *Najważniejsze misje izraelskich tajnych służb,* Rebis, Poznań, 2012.

Beaumont P., *Was Israeli raid a dry run for attack on Iran?,* in: "The Observer", 16.09.2007.

Biziewski J., Kubiak K., *Jom Kippur,* Altair, Warsaw, 1995.

Bogdański M., *MiG-29 w Polsce,* in: "Aeroplan" Issue No. 5–6/2006.

Cebulok P., *Izraelskie Siły Lotnicze – Historia i teraźniejszość,* in: "Nowa Technika Wojskowa", Issue No. 11/1995.

Czajkowski N., Sałata D., Sałata K., Wrona A., *Polskie MiGi w Izraelu,* in: "Skrzydlata Polska", Issue No. 05/2012.

Dunstan S., *The Six Day War 1967*: Sinai, Osprey 2009.

Efrati Y., *Colors & markings of the Israeli Air Force,* Isra Decals, Israel, 2005.

Fetke F., Izak K., review of M. Bar-Zohar, *Najważniejsze misje izraelskich tajnych służb,* Rebis, Poznań, 2012, in: "Przegląd bezpieczeństwa wewnętrznego" Issue No. 8/2013.

Fiszer M., Gruszczyński J., *F-16 Jastrząb,* Magnum-X, Warsaw, 2006.

Fiszer M., Gruszczyński J., *Historia i współczesność Wojskowych Zakładów Lotniczych nr 2 S.A., in*: "Lotnictwo LAI", Issue No. 5/2016.

Gajzler M., *Northrop F-5A/B Freedom Fighter,* Part 1 andin 2: "Lotnictwo", Issue No. 3–4/2016.

Gordon Y., Dexter K., Komissarov D., *Mikoyan MiG-21,* Midland, UK, 2008.

Gordon Y., Gunston B., *MiG-21 Fishbed,* Aerofax, Leicester, UK, 1996.

Gotowała J., *Lotnictwo we współczesnych konfliktach zbrojnych 1945–2003,* Bellona, Warsaw, 2004.

Gruszczyński J., Fiszer M., *Mikojan – MiG-21F-13,* Part 2, in: "Lotnictwo", Issue No. 12/2008.

Gruszczyński J., Mikutel T., Rybak E.F., Piotrowski C., Gretzyngier R, *MiG-21,* "Przegląd Konstrukcji Lotniczych" series No. 25, Altair, Warsaw, 1995.

Gruszczyński J., Rybak E. F., *F-15 Eagle,* Magnum-X, Warsaw, 2001.

Gruszczyński J., Rybak E. F., Piotrowski C., Wasielewski M., *MiG-23 Wersje myśliwskie,* Magnum-X, Warsaw, 1999.

Grzegorzewski J., *Samolot bombowy Tu-16,* Bellona, Warsaw, 2000.

Grzegorzewski J., Skierski Z., *Nowoczesna broń lotnicza,* MON, Warsaw, 1984.

Gunston B. M., Spick M., *Modern air combat,* Salamander Books, London, 1983.

Hersh S. M., *A Strike in the Dark,* in: "The New Yorker", 11.02.2008.

Hess P., *White House says Syria 'must come clean' about nuclear work,* in: "The Associated Press", 25.04.2008.

Hill D. (ed.), *Kronika wojen,* collective work, AKA, Głuchołazy, 2009.

Israelis 'blew apart Syrian nuclear cache', in: "The Sunday Times", 16.09.2007.

Jońca A., *Barwa w lotnictwie polskim,* Pt. 5 "Samoloty linii lotniczych 1957–1981", WKŁ, Warsaw, 1986.

Kaczkowski R., *Samolot PZL-104 Wilga,* WKŁ, Warsaw, 1983.

Konieczny J. R., *Samolot transportowy An-12,* "Typy Broni i Uzbrojenia" series No. 23, MON, Warsaw, 1973.

Kowal R., *Rozmowy ze zdrajcą,* Internovator, Warsaw, 1998.

Królikiewicz T., Gretzyngier R., *Polski samolot i barwa 1943–2016,* Bellona, Warsaw, 2016.

Kubiak, K. *Wojna falklandzka 1982,* AJ-Press, Gdańsk, 2002.

Kwas R., Gołembiewski M., *IAI Kfir,* AJ-Press, Gdańsk, 1996.

Lenartowicz T., *100 lat przygody Mielca z lotnictwem,* Mielec, 2015.

Liwinski J., *Transport lotniczy w Polsce w okresie międzywojennym*, in: "Lotnictwo", Issue No. 10/2008.
Makowski W., *Cywil w wojsku – wspomnienia z życia i wojen*, ZP, Warsaw, 2012.
MiG-21PF, in: "Magazyn Modelarski Payo", Issue No. 1/2009.
MiGiem w XX wiek, in: "Skrzydlata Polska", Issue No. 01/1993.
Mikołajczuk M., Gruszczyński J., *MiG-25RB niezwykły czterdziestolatek*, Pt.2, *in*: "Lotnictwo", Issue No. 7/2010.
Mikulski M., Glass A., *Polski transport lotniczy 1918–1978*, WKŁ, Warsaw, 1980.
Nicolle D., Cooper T., *Arab MiG-19 and MiG-21 units in combat*, Osprey, UK, 2004.
Poray A., *Pierwsza wojna libańska, Pt. 2*, in: "Skrzydlata Polska", Issue No. 3/2010.
Pospišil M., Stolár M. J., *Siły Powietrzne i Kosmiczne Sił Obronnych Izraela*, in: "Lotnictwo" Issue No. 1/2010.
Przymusiała P., *Haganah*, in: "Aero Technika Lotnicza", Issue Nos. 6 and 7/1990.
Przymusiała P., *MiG-21 na swiecie, Pt. 3*, in: "Aeroplan", Issue No. 4/1996.
Radomyski A., *Gorące niebo nad Bliskim Wschodem, in*. Adam Marszałek, Toruń, 2007.
Rendall I., *Splash one: The story of jet combat*, W&N publ.1998, ISBN-13: 978-0297818526.
Rieszentikow W., *Na kursie bojowym*, L&L, Gdańsk, 2002.
Snatched: Israeli commandos 'nuclear' raid, in: "The Sunday Times", 23.10.2007.
Solarz J., *Doktryny militarne XX wieku*, Avalon, Kraków, 2009.
Spector I., *Loud and Clear: The Memoir of an Israeli Fighter Pilot*, Zenith Press 2009, ISBN 978-0-7603-3630-4.
Stafrace C., *Arab Air Forces*, Squadron-Signal, USA, 1994.
Stapfer H. H., *MiG-17 IN ACTION*, Squadron-Signal, USA, 1992.
Starface C., *Arab air forces*, Squadron-Signal, Texas, USA, 1994.
Syria blast 'linked to chemical weapons': report, Agence France-Presse (AFP), 19.09.2007.
Swanson A., Swanson M., Dougherty M. J., *Military Atlas of Air Warfare*, 2014 , ISBN 978-0-7858-3109-9.
Świątkiewicz B., *Pod błękitną flagą*, Iskry, Warsaw, 1975.
Zabłocki E., *Siły powietrzne*, AON, Warsaw, 2007.
Zabłocki E., *Współczesne siły powietrzne*, AON, Warsaw, 2002.
Zaloga S. J., *Unmanned aerial vechicles*, Osprey, UK, 2008.
Zbiegniewski A., *MiG-i z bazy 228*, in: "Aero", Issue No. 6–7/2007.

Websites

13 maja 1977 – Zapomniany lot 6883 do Bejrutu, "Krakowski Oddział Stowarzyszenia Seniorów Lotnictwa Wojskowego RP", http://www.kosslwrp.republika.pl/www/html/historia.htm.
Cooper, T. *Israeli-Syrian Shadow-Boxing.*, ACIG, 30 September 2003; http://www.acig.info/CMS/.
Cooper T., *Suez Crisis 1956*, ACIG 2009, http://www.acig.info/CMS/.
Cooper T., *Suez Crisis, 1956: The War of Stripes*, ACIG 2009, http://www.acig.info/CMS/.
Israel downed 2 Syrian MiGs in 2001, WorldTribune.com, 2005, http://www.worldtribune.com/worldtribune/05/breaking2453413.05625.html.
Lenartowicz T., *Moje życie i samolot – co mechanik wie o lotnictwie*, http://cowiemechanikolotnictwie.blogspot.com.
Luto K., *Aeronautics Defense "Orbiter"*, http://www.samolotypolskie.pl/samoloty/226/126/Aeronautics-Defense-Orbiter2.
Musella M., *Air Operations During The 1973 Arab-Israeli War And The Implications For Marine Aviation*, Marine Corps Command and Staff College 1985, www.globalsecurity.org/military/library/report/1985/MML.htm.
Officials say Israel raid on Syria triggered by arms fears, Reuters 2007, http://uk.reuters.com/article/uk-syria-israel-targets-idUKSCH23352020070912.
Polskie F-16 w Izraelu, Altair 17.04.2015, http://www.altair.com.pl/news/view?news_id=7512.
Poms S., *The aircraft that fell in the hands of the IAF throughout the years have answered some questions regarding the enemies' capabilities*, 2015, http://www.iaf.org.il/4418-44740-en/IAF.aspx.
Semczuk P., *1977 Zapomniany lot 6883*, "Newsweek", 01.12.2009, http://historia.newsweek.pl/1977-zapomniany-lot-6883,49643,1,1.html.
US accuses Syria of building secret reactor with NKorea's help, 2008, http://web.archive.org/web/20110520132008/http://afp.google.com/article/ALeqM5jWIBgbzyBkHnJzQeMi80gXfjX0-Q.
Wojciechowski M.,*MiG-29*, http://www.mig.mariwoj.pl/mig-29-pl.htm.